Architectural Guide
Berlin

Architectural Guide Berlin

Dominik Schendel

With further contributions by
Philipp Meuser and Martin Püschel

Translated by Clarice Knowles

DOM
publishers

Contents

Photo: Jasmine Deng

Photo: iStockphoto/Holger Mette

Photo: Jasmine Deng

Photo: Jasmine Deng

Photo: Erik-Jan Ouwerkerk

© Peter Leibing, Hamb

Photo: Hans-Erich Bogatzky

On the Trail of the Berlin Wall
Page 88–117

On the Trail of *Plattenbau*
Page 118–183

Photo: Paul Meuser

Photo: Paul Meuser

Tour C: **Two hours by bicycle**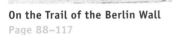

Tour D: **Three hours by car**

Photo: Erik-Jan Ouwerkerk

City model of Berlin: there is always work to be done!

Rediscover Architecture!

Philipp Meuser

What is the state of play regarding architectural criticism?

After the fall of the Berlin Wall in 1989 with the international architectural elite standing in line before the gates of the city, the air in Berlin was suffused with the optimism of planners and the utopianism of their ideas. Scarcely a week would go by without some superstar presenting their designs for Berlin in packed venues. Planning was running rampant, building work was going on everywhere and discussions were intense and plentiful. Architecture – so went the mantra of the 1990s – had become a catalyst for the city's new identity, an identity which left the trauma of car-oriented urban planning in the East and West far behind, accepted the historic city plan as at best a benchmark for new ideas and allowed Berlin architecture to link in the circle of European metropolises once more. A generation has since passed. The 1990s are history and one may fondly recall those "good old days," when commending one or other architectural language was tantamount to a declaration of beliefs. However, after the turn of the millennium verbal skirmishes over the monopoly on interpretation of architecture were succeeded by a certain reticence of opinion.
Today, well-intentioned exhibitions by institutions based in Berlin and their grassroots democratic selection panels regrettably contain a single rather meagre message: look here – we in Berlin also build houses! The new airport, which has been delayed for years, and the controversial reconstruction of the City Palace in particular ensure that architecture has been relegated to a lower middle ranking within societal acceptance. Upon completion of these large-scale buildings, a particular degree of tact and skill must be applied to transform the public perception of these fiscal high-risk projects into architectural masterpieces. Both have the potential.
However, there are no grounds for panic – the discipline of architectural critique is not faced with one of its worst crises, even if daily newspapers scarcely devote enough space to architecture, something deserving of it and which should have been given a permanent presence within the cityscape. Following the cycle of architectural debates in German history, a substantial discussion on the role of architecture in German society may be expected as early as 2023. It will then be exactly thirty years since Vittorio Magnago Lampugnani opened up the Berlin debate which spread like wildfire. In an article in *Der Spiegel*, Germany's leading weekly political magazine, the urban theoretician emphasised at the time that, "When you cannot quickly rid an area of a building when it is no longer pleasing to the eye you have to look for something fresh, some quality which doesn't look weary but also doesn't just pander to current fashion. This can only be an aesthetics of simplicity, clarity and serenity – an aesthetics of order, into the void of which each individual may project his or her own dreams."

What happened to patina?

That which was designed at the time now looks somewhat shabby in places. The desired patina failed to materialise for most of the once highly praised façades. Instead of that, the buildings have changed ownership (in any case anonymous) several times, broken stone slabs offer a glimpse of cavities accommodating cable ducts and the thermal insulation alike, when even the façades are simply dirty. The simplicity discussed so vehemently back then has yielded to disillusionment in many parts.

Plan by Hans Scharoun in 1946: an emptied city centre bisected by thoroughfares

Monotony and lack of ideas – as forecasted by critics earlier – have become an unintended reality at Pariser Platz (Paris Square). Examples which really did succeed can be whittled down to roughly three dozen. This sobering truth inevitably recalls the verdict of the architectural critic Rainer Haubrich who, as early as 1999, wrote, "Contemporary architecture does not have to solely produce something unprecedented. Truly contemporary architecture is a response to the perceived shortcomings of predecessors." Young architects have shown what this may entail for almost ten years. Expressive sculpture-like building designs have emerged primarily within privately financed residential construction, although these could just as much be located in Copenhagen, Amsterdam or Vienna. If the "Berlinish" in architecture was being debated in the 1990s, the elegant new buildings in Mitte, Prenzlauer Berg or Charlottenburg appear as an antithesis to Berlin in the period directly after reunification.

What does the young generation have to say?

As colleagues in Germany agonised over a *Berlinische Architektur*[1] (Berlinish Architecture), the author of this architectural guide was still attending kindergarten, making notes on architecture in wax crayon at best. Dominik Schendel is thus representative of a new generation of architectural critique. His approach to

architecture is free of ideology. His critique begins with the selection of a building. His texts are decidedly factual and neutral, steering clear of any controversy. Complementing his three chapters is a tour which Martin Püschel assisted in the completion of. Thus, a well-composed architectural guide has been created which draws the reader's attention to the unique features of Berlin's architectural history. The former division of the city is reflected in two chapters: *The Former East: Unter den Linden* and *The Former West: Kurfürstendamm*. The route outlined in the third chapter is also typical of Berlin's history: *On the Trail of the Berlin Wall*. The fourth chapter similarly addresses a topic which is best observed in Berlin: *On the Trail of Plattenbau*. Therefore, a brief excerpt of Berlin's inexhaustible past relating to building activity is reflected in 100 short texts.

What can Berlin learn from history?

Looking back on urban development since the fall of the Wall, individual buildings may be disappointing. Although the most prestigious architects of our time realised their designs next to the Spree, the result is relatively sobering. This may be due in part to the rapid development and planning pressure which arose therefrom, which the reunification of the city involved. Another reason may be the nature of today's construction output, in which decisions on architectural details

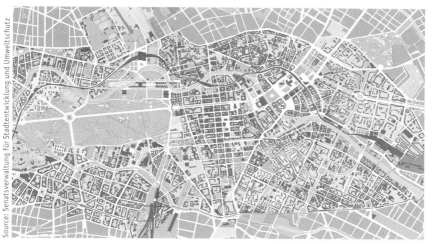

Source: Senatsverwaltung für Stadtentwicklung und Umweltschutz

Plan by Hans Stimmann in 1996: reconstructed urban layouts and redensification wherever one looks

are often no longer taken by the architect, but rather the project manager. However, Berlin has exemplary features to offer on an international scale in another aspect. Here, the emphasis is placed on something we take for granted which is only comprehensible to experts and insiders: the discipline of urban design which, owing to terminological imprecision, is often equated with urban planning. In this context, it may be a twist of fate that Berlin's new cityscape is only defined by the sum of individual buildings – which closely resembles the concept of urban development. Although Paris and London focus on the media impact of solitary buildings, Berlin is conspicuous by the ordinary. The latter should not necessarily be equated with mediocrity. Berlin is among those cities whose appearance has continuously changed in past centuries. It is also among those German cities which have repeatedly undergone the most prominent transformations as a result of planning. Each new political or economic upheaval brings with it a clearance of the old city in favour of a new and allegedly better societal model: Baroque Berlin made way for modern commercial buildings, hotels and government buildings at the end of the nineteenth century in the *Gründerzeit* (Berlin's founding era). In the period of the 1920s, modernist urban visions were to replace a Berlin made of stone. Protagonists of each movement, such as Ludwig Hilberseimer, who proposed at the time the demolition

of the historic Friedrichstadt, made their mark, albeit only in theory. Indeed, ideas proposing the destruction of the city were taken seriously only a few years later. Albert Speer devised an expansive north-south axis across Berlin in the time of National Socialism, although the Second World War put an end to these plans. Following the division of the city into East and West Berlin, the socialist capital of the GDR with wide thoroughfares and large marching grounds was developed on the one side and the democratic window display of the West featuring motorways and a city along American lines on the other. Significantly, the first plan – which was drawn up for the entire city following the Second World War – was a network of thoroughfares which blanketed the city like a net. It was established under the leadership of Hans Scharoun in 1946 and went down in architectural history as the *Kollektivplan* (Collective Plan). Especially after 1945, Berlin was the city – owing to its role as the capital in the Third Reich – with a particularly strong desire to wipe out politically contaminated buildings and the historic city plan. Architects and the post-war generation of building planners worked in both the East and the West to oppose their own history and with a belief in technical progress.

After the war had left the city in ruins, radical concepts could be set in concrete without taking into account the historic city plan. In contrast to similar processes in other German cities, Berlin was the scene for an ambitious urban and architecture ideological competition in the decades of German division. The common thread uniting the competing systems was the conscious infliction of damage to the architecture and the existing layout of the streets and squares alike, as well as the full-fledged demolition of historic buildings.

With the dawn of a new era, the Berlin of the past was also set to transform into a new – in any event car-oriented – city aligned with the political alignment of the time. This initially began in East Berlin with the foundation of the GDR in 1949 and the State's uninhibited use of private land made possible by collectivisation. The new urban design focused on the design for the power base of the GDR around the site of the City Palace – which was demolished in 1950 – and the old town to the east, as well as the planning of Stalinallee. For approximately three decades, Berlin was virtually dominated by a demolition euphoria in which the historic building fabric and medieval road networks were downright erased. The wounds remain visible today, particularly in the region between the Fernsehturm (TV Tower) and the Spreeinsel (Spree Island). Hardly anyone dares to speak of an old town. Memories have faded.

What is critical reconstruction?

At the beginning of the 1980s, Berlin conducted a reassessment of its architectural history with the Internationale Bauausstellung (International Building Exhibition, IBA) in West Berlin and the construction of the Nikolaiviertel (St. Nicholas' Quarter) in East Berlin. Modernity designed for traffic had already caused severe wounds in the form of thoroughfares, marching grounds and "greenery used to create distance". Owing to the strategy of repairing the urban fabric while restoring the traditional layout of the city and streets, Berlin was likewise a pioneer of gentle urban renewal and therefore an anticipated sustainable urban development. The path taken following German reunification continued

Source: Im Wandel beständig: Stadtumbau in Marzahn, 2007, p.40

The reality of Berlin in 2005: the demolition of vacant apartments in Marzahn-Hellersdorf

the concepts of the 1980s and drew conclusions from the history of demolition and destruction which took place in postwar modernism. In terms of urban development, this renewed transformation and modernisation was radically different from efforts made in the *Gründerzeit* at the turn of the twentieth century. Berlin explicitly committed itself to its urban and architectural history. Attempts were made to respect all aspects, successfully complete the modernisation process without major demolition and destruction and focus spatially on the inner urban development to prevent uncontrolled growth on the outskirts. In more general terms, the model of the European city with its strict division of public streets, squares and parks was put forward. Differing interpretations thus emerged on the basis of this urban concept, such as those by Heinz Hilmer and Christoph Sattler for Potsdamer and Leipziger Platz (Potsdam Square and Leipzig Square, 1991), Hans Kollhoff for Alexanderplatz (Alexander Square, 1993) or Bernd Albers for Friedrichswerder (2003). As diverse as the scale of these projects and the progress in implementing their architecture may be, they are nevertheless based on the fundamental principles of a European city. In terms of the specific building form, the architecture is modelled on abstract urban guidelines. The building is subordinate to the city, in the same manner as the private client must heed the public development plan.

The reality of Berlin in 2015: emergency shelters for refugees at Tempelhof Airport – the challenge for the next generation of architects lies in affordable housing

The provocation of the ordinary

Berlin may be a provocation for many critics. It is arguably the provocation of the ordinary, of natural architecture on the basis of an urban planning concept over 300 years of age, as in the case of Friedrichstadt. Berlin is certainly not a place where a new city has been devised after the fall of the Wall. Yet for those who wish to participate in an experiment related to tradition and history, Berlin is a premiere address in Europe. Berlin has also become a place where planning culture has changed in the last decade. Whereas occasionally the environment under the Senate Building Director, Hans Stimmann, was quite noisy, things were more tranquil – sometimes excessively so – under his successor. The convocation by Regula Lüscher from Switzerland will be hailed as a new chapter in the architectural history of Berlin. All parties involved are brought around one table in cooperative panel discussions or asked in Internet forums to assist, the objective being to become an integral part of adjustment processes even prior to the planning. This means on the one hand less potential for conflict, but on the other also stifled the culture of debate. For what is there left to be debated in public when divergent positions have already been steered towards compromise before the project has even begun? There is enough material here to provoke

impassioned debate. The new cornerstone of urban construction is to be created with above-average architecture in Europa City, north of the main train station, in contrast to the development south of the main train station. Berlin is to at last be given a striking silhouette on Alexanderplatz with high-rises. The real challenge lies however in quotidian architecture, namely affordable housing. Since the debate about refugees in 2015 – when almost one million refugees came to Germany – architects and politicians have discussed a renaissance of social mass housing following years of neglect. This particularly applies to Berlin. Whereas in 2000 more than 100,000 apartments were left vacant and some were even demolished, the city has decided henceforth to build 20,000 apartments per year. By 2030, the number of inhabitants is expected to have risen from 3.6 to 3.8 million, pointing to incentives for both architecture and architectural critique.

Notes:
[1] The term is used for a specific Berlin architecture that historically stands out due to its purism, simplicity and clarity. See: For God's sake, not this kind of a capital. Heinrich Klotz in conversation with Nikolaus Kuhnert and Angelika Schnell, in: ARCH+ 122 (June 1994), p. 86.

The Former East:
Unter den Linden

Model façade for the reconstruction of the Stadtschloss
as the Humboldt-Forum (Franco Stella, 2019)

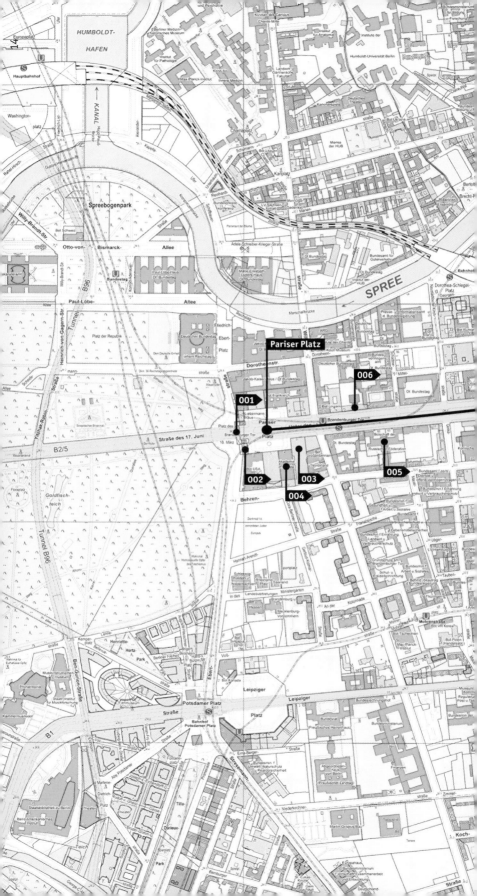

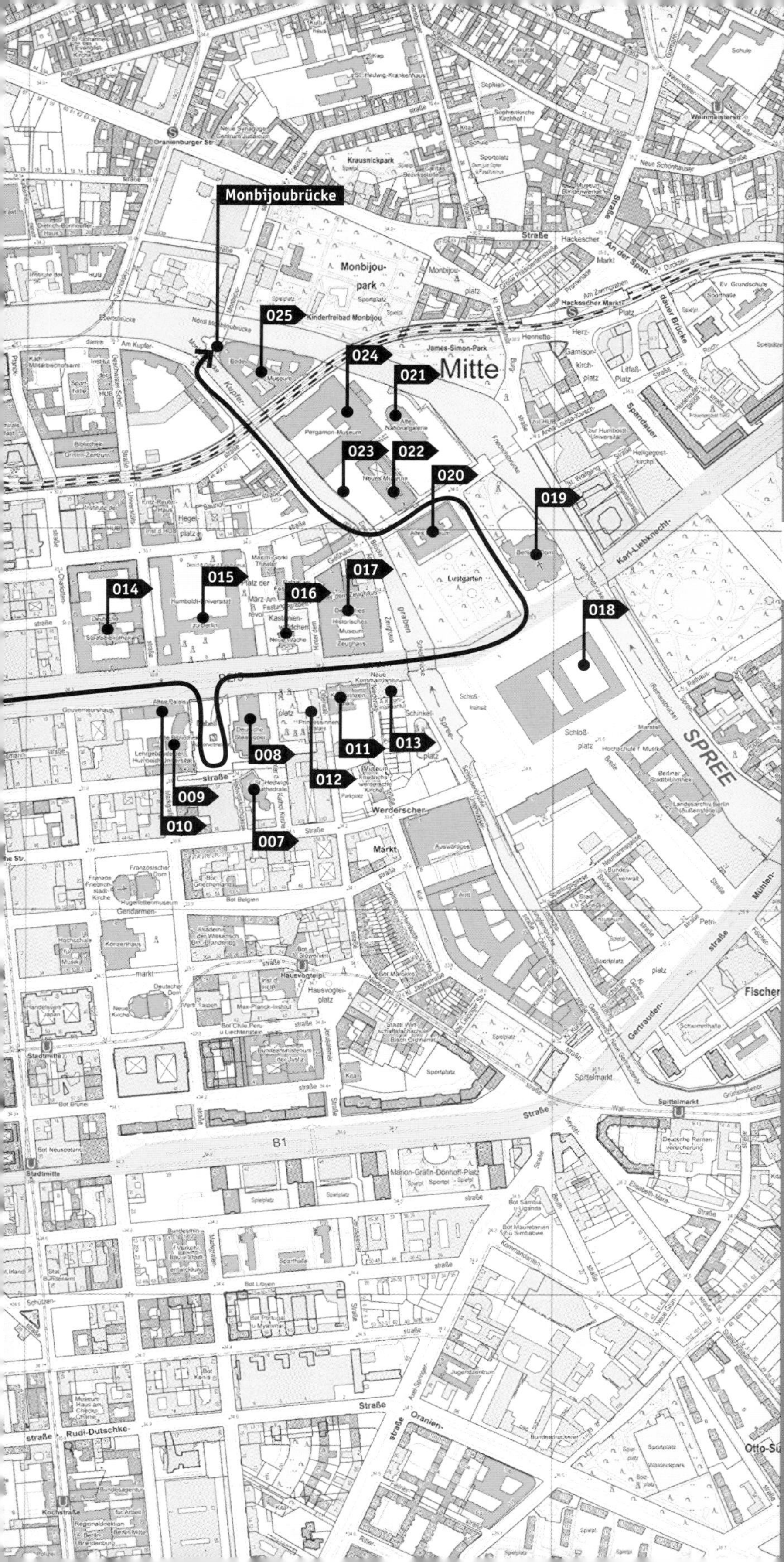

Monbijoubrücke

Monbijou-park

025

Kinderfreibad Monbijou

024

021

Mitte

023 022

Pergamon-Museum

Nationalgalerie

020

Neues Museum

019

014 015

016 017

018

008

011 013

009

012

010

007

SPREE

A

B1

Fischer

Otto-Su

Pariser Platz

002

001

002

View of the Brandenburger Tor and the
neighbouring grand boulevard Unter den Linden:
on the left in the foreground is the Tiergarten

014

006

005

04

A

Holocaust Memorial

2014

Ambassade de France

Embassy of Hungary

002

001

002

003

004

British Embassy

US Embassy

Holocaust Memorial

Romanian Embassy

Former Polish Embassy (006)

Russian Embassy Compound (005)

View from the south facing the western part of Unter den Linden: the Russian Embassy covers an area larger than the entire perimeter development of Pariser Platz

2011

014

009 010

015

007 008

016

012

011 017

013

020

Humboldt-Box

018 019

025

024

023

022

021

A

View of the Museumsinsel which has been a UNESCO World Heritage site since 1999

Brandenburger Tor

 A 001

Pariser Platz
Carl Gotthard Langhans
1791, 1868, 1957, 2002

The symbol of chequered German history has its origins in the Berlin Customs Wall which surrounded the garrison town of Berlin in the eighteenth century to prevent both desertions and the smuggling of goods. Most of the fourteen toll gates were named after the nearest cities within reach. In 1791, the "Soldier-King" Friedrich Wilhelm I commissioned the present-day gate to replace the modest toll station towards Brandenburg an der Havel. Langhans modelled it on the Propylaea in the Acropolis of Athens, with which he was familiar from published engravings. Leading to the city palace, the street Unter den Linden – which would evolve into a Prussian Via Triumphalis – thus received a fitting entrée and the burgeoning period of Prussian classicism also acquired its icon right from the outset. Six 15 m high Doric half-columns frame five passages, of which the broad central one was reserved for the King. Two flanking gatehouses originally provided accommodation for guardhouses and for toll collection. The paintwork feigning white marble was later replaced by brown and beige colour schemes, until today's appearance of stone surfaces asserted itself. In addition to the quadriga, other sculptural works can also be traced back to Johann Gottfried Schadow. The relief on the pedestal shows the procession of the goddess of peace, while the labours of Hercules are depicted in the passages. Statues of Mars, the god of war, and Minerva can be found in each side passage which only emerged after the Berlin Customs Wall came down. Following the victory over Napoleon and the repatriation of the quadriga – which had been abducted to Paris – Eirene, the goddess of peace, was adorned with a wreath of

Source: Deutsche Bauzeitung No. 84, 1906

A

**Haus Sommer and
Haus Liebermann**
Pariser Platz 1 and 7
Josef Paul Kleihues
1999

A 002

oak leaves, the Prussian eagle and the Iron Cross by Karl Friedrich Schinkel and was thus transformed into Victoria, the goddess of victory. In 1956 the bottom plaque, bullet-ridden from the Second World War, was rebuilt in West Berlin and handed over to the East Berlin city authorities who removed the emblems of Prussian-German militarism before placing the plaque on the restored gate. The emblems were added again after the fall of the Wall. The adjacent Liebermann and Sommer houses were built by Josef Paul Kleihues in the style of the former classical buildings by Friedrich August Stüler. When it came to the reconstruction, the gatehouses obtained porticoes located to the front and at the sides, which is why the gate stands freely today. The fact that the site is steeped in symbolism can also be seen from the names of Platz des 18. März (18 March Square) down to the west – which refers to the March Revolution of 1848 and the first free parliamentary elections in the GDR in 1990 – as well as Straße des 17. Juni (17 June Street), following the uprising in the GDR in 1953.

With the two houses on the left and right of Brandenburger Tor (Brandenburg Gate), Josef Paul Kleihues transferred his strategy of "critical reconstruction" from urban development to architecture. The houses were modelled on two mirror-image residential buildings which were extended in 1846 with classical alterations by Friedrich August Stüler, a pupil of Schinkel. Kleihues took an analysis of the proportions and formal details of the delicate plaster façades as a basis for his design. The result is strictly geometrical perforated façades with angular cornices, pediments and rustication, executed not in plaster, but rather in Portuguese sandstone. Unlike their archetypes, the new buildings are set back from the porticoes of the gate and, instead of the Stüleresque flat roof storey, receive one full floor, thus significantly misaligning the proportions. The façades are crowned by closed parapets and railings which break the symmetry of both buildings. The painter Max Liebermann lived in the precursor to the northern building until his death in 1935.

Hotel Adlon

Unter den Linden 75–77
Patzschke, Klotz & Partner
1997

A 003

In name, address and architecture the myth of the luxury hotel from 1907 is supposed to be evoked which Lorenz Adlon opened as a public stage for dinners and balls, following the American example. Wilhelm II supported the construction by enforcing the demolition of Schinkel's listed Palais Redern. The hotel was burnt down immediately after the end of the war. It was only in 1984 that the undamaged side wing was torn down. Carl Gause and Robert Leibnitz had originally created a building with a strongly vertically structured natural stone façade. The new building adopts the rusticated base, the circumferential balcony of the uppermost storey and the steep copper roof, although the composition of the sandstone and the plaster surfaces are in line with a classicism already deemed passé during the construction period of the original building. In comparison with the former Adlon, today's frontage is double as wide and 4 m higher. The edifice still seems stocky, in spite of the additional storey. The traditional hotel and the glass-deconstructivist academy illustrate the two opposing poles of the Berlin architectural dispute, although both are evidently children of their time.

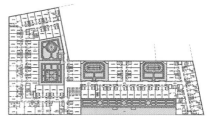

Photo: Stefan Liebrecht

Akademie der Künste

 A 004

Pariser Platz 4
Ernst von Ihne, Günter Behnisch,
Manfred Sabatke, Werner Durth
1906, 2005

A

The court architect Ernst von Ihne laid out the Palais Arnim in 1906 for the Akademie der Künste (Academy of Arts) and extended it by adding a wing dedicated to studios and exhibitions. As of 1937, the task force of Albert Speer, the General Building Inspector for the Redesign of the capital of the Reich, was housed here. Hitler was able to reach him through the ministerial gardens along Wilhelmstraße, unseen from the Reichskanzlei (Reich Chancellery), to gloat over models and plans. Following the war, GDR border troops used the exhibition wing which, since it was the only vestige of the prewar development, was not demolished. East and West German academies were to be merged at its historical location after the fall of the Wall. The design by Günter Behnisch, Manfred Sabatke and Werner Durth was the subject of one of the stormiest architectural debates in Berlin in the 1990s: stone or glass? The violation of the design guidelines for Pariser Platz (Paris Square), which stipulated the proportion of closed façades as well as their range of colours and materials, was only enforced with the partisanship of the German President Roman Herzog. Behnisch was able to create a façade made

of glass – a material which he was known to view as being intertwined with democratic values, such as openness and transparency. He placed a "storm" of inclined planes, walkways and flat glazed surfaces around the historic exhibition rooms. The requirements for historical preservation – namely to maintain the entire traditional inventory of the only preserved building on Pariser Platz – were not complied with. The demolition of the side small rooms from 1906, the additional storeys, conversions and extensions by Albert Speer and the fittings made in the GDR meant that the building lost a significant part of its historic dimensions.

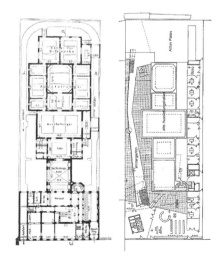

Source: Zentralblatt der Bauverwaltung, 1907, No. 71

Photo: Philipp Meuser

Russian Embassy

Unter den Linden 63–65
Anatoli Strischewski
1951

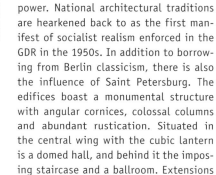
A 005

With the establishment of diplomatic relations, the Soviet Union sought to give the newly founded and sovereign (albeit to a limited extent) GDR the outward appearance of legitimacy. On the thirty-fifth anniversary of the October Revolution, the Soviet Embassy opened in 1952 in lieu of the war-ravaged Rococo palace, where the representative of the Russian Empire had resided since 1837. Adjacent plots were also added to the vast complex and an intersection overbuilt to allow for an impressive illustration of the prevailing balance of power. National architectural traditions are hearkened back to as the first manifest of socialist realism enforced in the GDR in the 1950s. In addition to borrowing from Berlin classicism, there is also the influence of Saint Petersburg. The edifices boast a monumental structure with angular cornices, colossal columns and abundant rustication. Situated in the central wing with the cubic lantern is a domed hall, and behind it the imposing staircase and a ballroom. Extensions were created in the 1960s and 1970s whereby, in addition to administrative rooms and civil servant apartments, other occupants such as the State-owned Aeroflot were also accommodated.

Photos: Philipp Meuser

Former Polish Embassy

Unter den Linden 70–72
Emil Leybold, Christian Seyfarth
1964

A

Following the Second World War, the embassies of socialist fraternal states replaced the largely destroyed civic development in the western section of the "Linden". In so doing, historic plots were amalgamated, although alignments and eaves' heights were maintained. A metal glazed façade with matt green balustrade areas was mounted on to the reinforced steel framework of the Embassy of Poland. A relief by Fritz Kühn adorns the entrance on the ground floor. A total of 244 stylised linden leaves made of steel are a reference to the location on Lindenallee. The embassy is to make way for a new building, in spite of the existing preservation order. The winning competition entry by Budzynski, Badowski and Kowalewski from 1998 proposed a complete conversion of the existing facilities.

After the Berlin senator of building and construction assessed the plans as being "not at all eligible for approval", these were revised three times before being completely discarded. Jems Architekten won a new competition in the year 2012. Outlined is a complex with several courtyards laid out in an irregular manner, a flat roof and a gridded natural stone façade, behind which the atrium extending the full height of the building emerges. The Polnische Kulturinstitut (Polish Cultural Institute) is set to move into the ground floor. GDR modernity had a difficult time after the fall of the Wall, not least because of the added exploitative pressures in relation to the increase in the permitted height of the eaves from 18 m to 22 m. The neighbouring Hungarian Embassy was demolished as early as 1999. The Lindencorso and the Unter den Linden hotel have also disappeared. Only the concrete frame of the GDR Ministry for People's Education on the corner of Wilhelmstraße remains intact.

1747: Georg Wenzeslaus von Knobelsdorff

 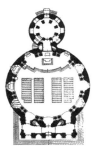

1887: Max Hasak

 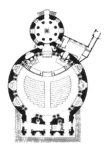

1932: Clemens Holzmeister

1963: Hans Schwippert

Photo: Philipp Meuser

St. Hedwigs-Kathedrale

Bebelplatz
Georg Wenzeslaus v. Knobelsdorff,
Joh. Boumann, Hans Schwippert
1773, 1963

A 007

Following the conquest of Catholic Silesia, the tolerant sovereign Friedrich the Great strove for inner unity. The construction of a Catholic church in Berlin was only possible after the Reformation. In keeping with the instructions of Friedrich, the design by Georg Wenzeslaus von Knobelsdorff is based on the Pantheon. Johann Boumann created the rotunda in sober rusticated plaster. The sandstone portico with its six colossal pilaters is located diagonal to Bebelplatz (Bebel Square). It was not until the nineteenth century that the soprapforte and tympanum reliefs were created from designs by Georg F. Ebenhech.

The establishment of the diocese of Berlin led to St. Hedwig becoming its cathedral in 1930. Almost the entire church was burnt down in 1943. Hans Schwippert dispensed with the lantern subsequently placed atop and reestablished the original proportions as part of the reconstruction effort prior to 1963. Under the new concrete shell construction, the upper and lower churches are linked effectively by a generous opening with a glazed balustrade and wide staircase. Furthermore, the altar column combines both levels. The opening unfortunately prevents the congregation gathering around the altar. A 2014 award-winning design by Sichau & Walter Architekten and Leo Zogmayer aims to revamp the interior by proposing the conversion of Schwippert's listed version and the closure of the central opening.

2014: Zogmayer/Sichau & Walter Architekten

Condition ca. 1900

Photo: Max Lautenschläger

Staatsoper

Unter den Linden 7
Georg W. von Knobelsdorff et al.
1742, 1786, 1844, 1955, 2017

A 008

Even as a young crown prince, Friedrich II had already completed the first sketches of the Forum Fridericianum and the opera house with his then art teacher, Knobelsdorff. The Hofoper (Court Opera) is considered to be the first freestanding theatre not to have been integrated into a castle. The monumental and palatial frontage confronted the armoury of the Zeughaus – a symbol of the military by which Prussian rulers traditionally demonstrated their power – in a self-confident manner and as a cultural sign of the Enlightenment. At first

all spectators were guests of the King. As a rule, the performance of an opera was merely a component of a courtly festivity. The hall featuring a stage and spectator gallery could thus be interconnected for balls. The Apollosaal (Apollo Hall) served as a foyer and banquet hall. Knobelsdorff accentuated the main façade with a temple-like portico which is rooted in the tradition of Palladian villas. Following a total of five major conversions and renovations (!), it is the only component which has largely remained in its original state. As early as 1786, the building was for the first time adapted to meet increasing demands as regards comfort and stage technology. In 1843 it was burnt down to its foundation walls. The opera was bombed out

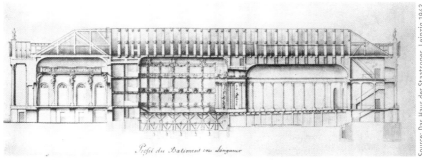

Source: Das Haus der Staatsoper, Leipzig 1942

Section through the original room sequence of the Apollosaal (foyer and banquet room), Theatersaal (spectator gallery and ballroom) and Korinthischer Saal (stage and concert hall)

Source: HG Merz

Interior of the Staatsoper Unter den Linden following the renovation by HG Merz (2017)

A

during the Second World War and reconstructed in record time which served as an effective propagandistic tool – only to be destroyed again after barely a year. When it was reconstructed for the second time in 1955, Richard Paulick reduced the height of the stage tower and redesigned the interiors to conform with Knobeldorff's original form. This was also in line with the ideology of national traditions of architecture. Paulick spent four months in the Schloss Sanssouci (Sanssouci Castle) with thirty employees to analyse Knobeldorff's vocabulary. The internal and external shapes again merge into a harmonious whole. After the fall of the Wall, the ailing building failed to satisfy the requirements governing an opera house as well as those with respect to accessibility, air-conditioning systems and fire safety measures. Klaus Roth's 2008 award-winning competition entry for the general refurbishment proposed a new spectator gallery in lieu of the traditional post-war version. The creation dating back to the early expansion phase of the GDR was evidently not yet commonly recognised as historically significant. After heated discussions and the veto by the governing mayor of Berlin, a new call for tenders stipulated the preservation of the hall. It has now been sensitively adjusted to enhance both visibility and acoustics under the direction of the Stuttgart-based architects HG Merz. As early as 2006, the architectural practice sensitively converted the Staatsrat (State Council) building,

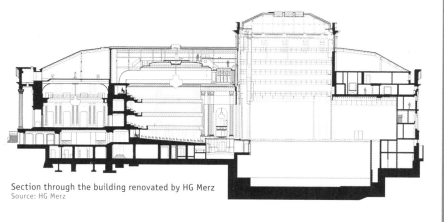

Section through the building renovated by HG Merz
Source: HG Merz

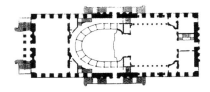

Source: Die Deutsche Staatsoper Berlin, 1971

1742: Georg Wenzeslaus v. Knobelsdorff

The opera house was primarily created as a setting for courtly festivities. After a performance, the King and court society were able to dine in the Apollosaal, while the floor of the auditorium was elevated to the height of the Korinthischer Saal – which had previously served as a stage – for the subsequent ball.

Source: Das Haus der Staatsoper und seine Baumeister, 1942

1788: Carl Gotthard Langhans

Its dual function as an opera house and a setting for festivities was swiftly abandoned owing to numerous restrictions imposed on stage operations. Langhans rebuilt the edifice, including its technical facilities. Realigned side boxes as well as an enlarged stage portal enhanced visibility.

Source: Zeitschrift für Bauwesen, No. 7, 1928

1844: Carl Ferdinand Langhans

The younger Langhans started to rebuild the opera house which had burnt down to its foundation walls after a fire. In so doing, he expanded the spectator gallery, inserted an additional fourth tier and moved the side risalits further outwards in favour of emergency exit stairs. The portico obtained a relief by Ernst Rietschel.

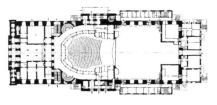

Source: Zeitschrift für Bauwesen, No. 7, 1928

1910

The edifice was expanded to the south as early as 1868 in order to mitigate the demand for space within the playhouse. This was followed in 1910 by side extensions and the installation of the fly-tower, required for modern operatic life. It was considered a stigma owing to its size and location offset from the side risalits.

1928: Eduard Fürstenau

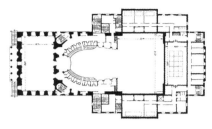

Source: Zeitschrift für Bauwesen, No. 7, 1928

After failed proposals for a new development and an unprecedented public debate, the stage tower was underpinned and the entire playhouse thus rebuilt in keeping with growing technical demands. The risalits wandered from the centre of the building to the front of the new side stages.

1942: Erich Meffert

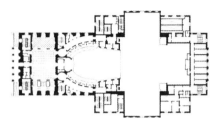

Source: Das Haus der Staatsoper und seine Baumeister, 1942

The bombed-out building was an effective propagandistic tool since it was reopened within the space of one year, midway through the war. The spectator gallery in the old geometry obtained a new décor. The Apollosaal was considerably reduced to improve the problematic accessibility situation.

A

1955: Richard Paulick

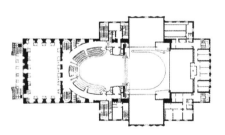

Source: Die Deutsche Staatsoper Berlin, 1971

The opera was bombed out once more as early as 1945. Paulick reduced the height of the stage tower by 5 m and redesigned the interior by taking into account Knobelsdorff's Rococo elements for the second reconstruction. The Apollosaal in its former size was modelled on the oval dining room in Schloss Sanssouci.

2017: HG Merz

Source: Senatsverwaltung für Stadtentwicklung

At the start of the general renovation work, little more than the front facing Lindenallee remained of the fabric of the original building. HG Merz maintains the cubature, floor plan and décor dating back to 1955. The raising of the hall ceiling in favour of a whispering gallery, as a senstive modification, is hardly visible.

The former depot building following the renovation by HG Merz and rw+ (2016)

a GDR masterpiece, and the Staatsbibliothek zu Berlin (State Library of Berlin) on Unter den Linden within walking distance, as well as renovating the depot building of the Staatsoper (State Opera) in the direct vicinity. To this end, the ceiling panelling and the proscenium were raised 5 m and a whispering gallery inserted above the third tier. The hall will be in Paulick's original colour scheme following the conversion. In future, opposites will collide in the depot building on Französische Straße. Although the membrane of the former depot will be renovated by HG Merz and rw+ in the GDR style of the *Nationale Tradition* (National Tradition), the Pierre-Boulez-Konzertsaal (Pierre Boulez Concert Hall) with its 622 seats in two ring-shaped tiers gives rise to a political statement of an architectural nature.

Central stage in the Pierre-Boulez-Saal (2016)

Daniel Barenboim commissioned a concert hall for his globally recognised West-Eastern Divan Orchestra in the building complex to the east of the Staatsoper. The American architect Frank O. Gehry designed an amorphous inner life as a token of friendship.

Interior of the Barenboim-Said-Akademie according to a design by Frank O. Gehry (2016)

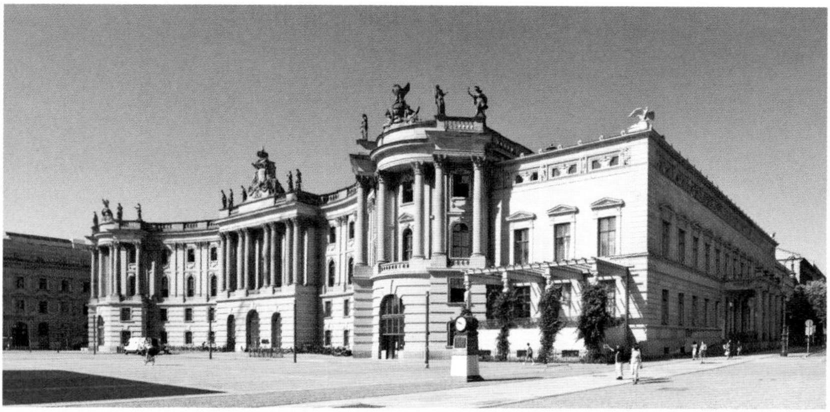

Alte Bibliothek ≈ A 009

Bebelplatz 1
Georg Christian Unger et al.
1780, 1969

Friedrich the Great authorised Georg Christian Unger and Michael Philipp Boumann to design the new building for the royal book collection in the style of the Baroque Michaelertrakt (St. Michael's Wing) of the Hofburg palace in Vienna. The first library building in Berlin owes its nickname – "chest of drawers" – to the concave façade. Central and corner risalits protrude with colossal Corinthian columns above the high base. In 1914, the collection was moved to the other side of Unter den Linden when it was still the Preußische Staatsbibliothek (Prussian Royal Library). After the war, the façade overlooking the square was rebuilt by Werner Kötteritzsch. Behind arose a new building for Humboldt-Universität (Humboldt University). Micha Ulman's *Versunkene Bibliothek* (*Sunken Library*) in the middle of Bebelplatz (Bebel Square) commemorates under a glazed panel the book burning carried out by the National Socialists.

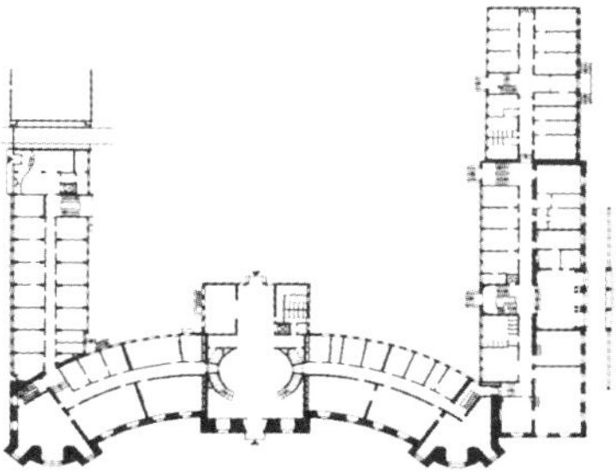

Source: Berlin. Architektur von Pankow bis Köpenick, 1987

Altes Palais ≈ A 010

Unter den Linden 9
Carl Ferdinand Langhans et al.
1837, 1964, 2005

Langhans built the city palace of the Prussian crown prince based upon the narrow side of the prominent Alte Bibliothek (Old Library). Even when he was Emperor of Germany, Wilhelm I. preferred the palace as a place of residence and base of operations to the city castle. His workspaces were situated to the left of the portico-like forecourt, above those of his wife Augusta. Wilhelm observed the changing of the guards on a daily basis from the corner window of his room – an event which quickly found mention in travel guides. The complex, with its wings situated within a leafy courtyard, originally extended to Behrenstraße. The sober two-storey plaster façade with sandstone structuring culminates in an attic, whose square windows, terracotta statues and coats of arms by Ludwig Wichmann lend it structure. It was not until 1964 that the palace, together with the Alte Bibliothek, was rebuilt with a different spatial planning system and storey height after the destruction caused by the Second World War. Owing to the extension of the adjacent Oranische Gasse (Oranian Lane) with the Baroque Gouverneurshaus (Governor's House), the palace is no longer free-standing facing the street. In 2007, the leafy pergola on Bebelplatz (Bebel Square) was also rebuilt following the restoration of the ascending eagles at the building corners and of the original colour scheme.

Kronprinzenpalais ☆   A 011

Unter den Linden 3
Philipp Gerlach, Johann H. Strack,
Karl Friedrich Schinkel et al.
1663, 1732, 1811, 1857, 1970

Prinzessinnenpalais ☆   A 012

Unter den Linden 5
Friedrich Wilhelm Diterichs,
Heinrich Gentz et al.
1730, 1733, 1811, 1964

Built in 1663, the private house served as the official residence of the Governor of Berlin from 1706 and was converted by Philipp Gerlach for the Prussian Crown Prince Friedrich into a Baroque palace with a central risalit in 1732. After the hitherto unknown Schinkel had redesigned several rooms, he was commissioned with a connecting arch to the Prinzessinnenpalais (Princesses' Palace). In the year 1857, Johann H. Strack replaced the mansard roof by a third storey and remodelled the façade with classic décor, maintaining the colossal pilasters and massive cornice. The entrance ramp has a high porch. An asymmetrical sixth axis facing the street was removed and extended behind to form a wing. A colonnade denotes the plot boundary. The Royal Family resided in the building prior to 1918. Following the demise of the monarchy, the Neue Abteilung (New Department) of the Nationalgalerie (National Gallery) in Berlin emerged here as the first museum of contemporary art. The war-damaged building was demolished in the year 1961. In common with the Prinzessinnenpalais, Richard Paulick continued reconstructing the exterior of the palace until 1970. The two-storey east wing was also restored to have three storeys. The interior was redesigned as the guesthouse of the East Berlin city authorities, where the reunification treaty was signed in 1990. Today it is an exhibition space and events forum.

Two private houses on Oberwallstraße were combined as early as three years after their establishment by Friedrich Wilhelm Diterichs to become a palace for the Prussian Minister of Finance. The street façade was unified and fitted with a risalit featuring four Ionian pilasters, a balcony and a flight of steps. Owned by the House of Hohenollern as of 1811, the palace was integrated within the streetscape between the opera and the Kronprinzenpalais (Crown Princes' Palace) through a classical reception building by Heinrich Gentz. The daughters of the King and other members of the royal household initially resided in the palace. The Schinkel-Museum has resided here since 1931. Almost twenty years following damage incurred during the war, the ramshackle ruins were demolished after measurements and castings had been produced beforehand. Richard Paulic continued until 1964 to create a new building which externally corresponded to the original building, incorporating the wrought-iron Rococo railings from the castle demolished in 1964. These are also the work of Diterich. The garden was created in 1740 and has been made accessible to the public. It is furnished with a café terrace. The three bronze generals from the Wars of Liberation against Napoleon are the work of Christian Daniel Rauch and were banished in the GDR from their original place of honour on the street to the depths of the garden.

Kommandantenhaus

Unter den Linden 1
Rupert and York Stuhlemmer,
Thomas van den Valentyn
2003

Bertelsmann AG acquired the property located at the prominent address of Unter den Linden 1 following the demolition in 1995 of the elongated high-rise of the East German Foreign Ministry parallel to the Kupfergraben. The obligation to accurately reconstruct the exterior of the Kommandantenhaus (Commander's House), whose wartime ruins were torn down in the year 1950, was a prerequisite for the acquisition. The original building was created by Friedrich Wilhelm Titel in 1796 as a two-storey Baroque palace with

a hipped roof. The place of residence and base of operations for the military commander of Berlin was extended between 1873 and 1874 and received a façade design with abundant plaster rustication like a Florentine palace. Eight ascending eagles made of terracotta accentuate the eaves. Although Rupert and York Stuhlemmer faithfully reconstructed the façades, the emphatically contemporary interior is the work of Thomas van den Valentyn. The reconstruction of the recessed middle area of the rear façade was abandoned for the sake of a steel and glass structure. Seven brick formats derived from the various formative stages of the original building were used in the restoration of the façades. This was based on a cartographic photograph, rectified amateur photographs, a historic cadastral map and the exposed foundations. The front garden situated on the public pavement constituted an exception on the grand boulevard from the outset. Levin Monsigny have redesigned it in the form of two semi-circles.

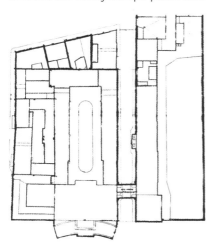

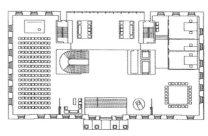

View into the reading room of the Staatsbibliothek:
a cubic body of light soars above a base consisting of bookshelves

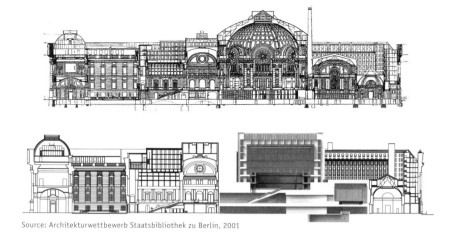

Source: Architekturwettbewerb Staatsbibliothek zu Berlin, 2001

Staatsbibliothek ☒ ↵

Unter den Linden 8
Ernst von Ihne, HG Merz
1914, 2016

A 014

Between 1903 and 1914, Ernst von Ihne created the new building for the growing Königliche Bibliothek (Royal Library) in lieu of the Baroque stables. The university library and Akademie der Wissenschaften (Academy of Sciences) were, to begin with, also incorporated into the enormous complex covering an area of 170 m x 107 m. Seven inner courtyards illuminate the quad. Lurking behind the sandstone façade, whose rusticated base and two main storeys lend it structure, are as many as thirteen storeys containing books which are designed as supporting steel shelves. The sequence of Lindenhalle (Linden Hall), the court of honour, the stairway hall and the vestibule culminates

in the central reading room, whose dome with a span of 38 m was larger than that of the Berliner Dom (Berlin Cathedral). This was severely damaged in the Second World War and was later replaced by repository towers. After the fall of the Wall, the book inventories of the Staatsbibliothek (State Library) in East and West Berlin were combined again, whereby historical research was housed in the original building on Unter den Linden and the collections of the modern period in Scharoun's building at the Kulturforum (Cultural Forum) in West Berlin. HG Merz restored the original striking room sequence as part of the general restoration work. A large new reading room, whose cubic body of light soars above a base consisting of bookshelves, emerged as a functional and effective focal point. Three layers of glass and the translucent textile membrane are used for the light control.

Humboldt-Universität ⌃

Unter den Linden 6
Johann Boumann et al.
1753, 1920, 1962

A 015

Friedrich the Great had initially planned a residential castle at this location on the grand boulevard. Instead, a city palace was built for his brother Heinrich. The master builder Johann Boumann presumably fell back on Knobelsdorff's plans, the latter having fallen from grace. The three-sided court of honour continues into the neighbouring Bebelplatz (Bebel Square) to the north. In 1809, the Prinz Heinrich Palais (Prince Heinrich Palace) was given over to the newly founded university. Between 1913 and 1920, the town surveyor Ludwig Hoffmann extended the building at the back to include two elongated wings in similar forms. After the destruction by war, it continued to be rebuilt until 1962. Neo-classical furnishings were installed inside. Today's figures above the side risalits of the edifice hail from Potsdamer Stadtschloss (Potsdam City Palace) which has been demolished.

A

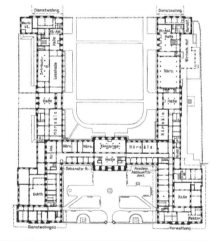

Bauten, part V, 2004

Neue Wache

Unter den Linden 4
Karl Friedrich Schinkel,
Heinrich Tessenow et al.
1818, 1931, 1993

A 016

Following the Wars of Liberation, Schinkel created the guardhouse of the Kronprinzenpalais (Crown Princes' Palace) as the first government building which, owing to the monumental Doric portico and the corner risalits, asserts itself among its larger neighbours. The cubic form with forceful angularity is borrowed from the Roman castrum. Schinkel used sculptural figures of Victory instead of triglyphs for the architrave at the front of the temple. In 1931, Heinrich Tessenow converted the guardhouse into a memorial to the fallen soldiers of the First World War. He removed the interior walls and intermediate ceilings and and filled in the windows on the brick side façades. A 2 m high granite block with a silver wreath of oak leaves was erected beneath an open oculus.

Severely damaged during the war, the building was renovated prior to 1960 as a memorial to the victims of fascism and militarism. It was furnished in 1969 with an eternal flame in a glass prism, in lieu of the granite block by Lothar Kwasnitza. It was opened in the year 1993 following the reunification as the central memorial of the Federal Republic of Germany with an enlarged replica of the bereaved mother figure by Käthe Kollwitz within the restored interior. The Kollwitz heirs insisted that the marble generals derived from Schinkel's concept (now opposite) by Christian D. Rauch never be displayed in front of the guardhouse again.

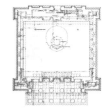

Sources: Die Neue Wache, 2011;
Berlin in der Geschichte seiner Bauten, 1960

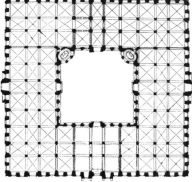

Source: istockphoto/Arpad Benedek

Zeughaus

Unter den Linden 2
Johann A. Nering, Martin Grünberg,
Andreas Schlüter et al.
1706, 1880, 1965

A 017

A

Four different master builders worked on the Zeughaus between 1695 and 1706. Today, the former armoury is the oldest building on Unter den Linden and, at the same time, one of the most prominent Baroque buildings in Berlin. The square courtyard is enclosed by four two-storey wings. Pilasters lend structure to the main area above the rusticated base. The façades, accentuated by a central risalit with Tuscan columns and tympanums, culminate in a balustrade featuring trophy ornamentation. In the inner courtyard, the twenty-two heads of dying warriors on the keystones of the ground floor are considered to be the pinnacle of Baroque sculpture in Prussia and were designed by Schlüter. The Zeughaus became a weapons museum following the establishment of the German Reich. In the year 1880, Friedrich Hitzig furbished the north wing with a hall of fame for the Prussian army and the courtyard with a glazed roof, a flight of stairs and a majestic statue of the national personification of Prussia: Borussia. The reconstruction effort was initially centred on the edifice's original state. However, static problems led to a complete gutting of the building. It was renovated prior to 1965 as the Deutsches Historisches Museum (German Historical Museum), whereby the interior – which Otto Häsler had newly arranged – was designed by Theodor Voissem with references to historic forms. The building has been the residence of the Deutsches Historisches Museum since 2003. Helmut Kohl personally commissioned I. M. Pei with the extension. A cubical form made of limestone accommodates workshops and exhibitions which are accessible via a glazed hall featuring a filigree stair cylinder at the tip of the site. The connection to the old building is underground.

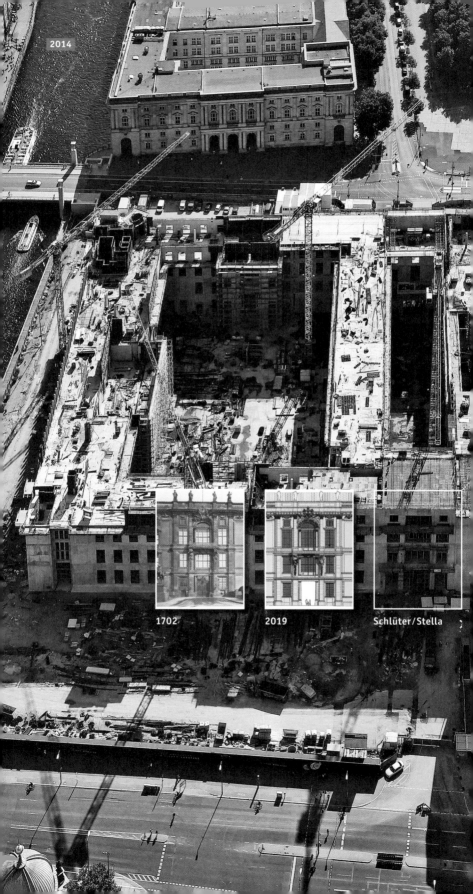

2014

1702   2019   Schlüter/Stella

1964 Korn

Humboldt-Forum

Schlossplatz
Franco Stella
2019

A 018

An association founded in 1992 by the Hamburg businessman Wilhelm von Boddien enforced the partial reconstruction of the Stadtschloss (City Palace) which had been demolished in the year 1950. Therefore the listed Palast der Republik (Palace of the Republic), in turn, was forced to give way. It was built by Heinz Graffunder in 1976 as the seat of the East German parliament, the Volkskammer

(People's Chamber), and a public cultural centre. The new Humboldt-Forum is intended to complement the Museums-insel (Museum Island) opposite with non-European collections from the Staat-liche Museen (State Museums), the sci-ence collection of Humboldt-Universität (Humboldt University) and part of the Zentralbibliothek (Central Library). The promotion of culture and science by cer-tain members of the Hohenzollern family offers the possibility of establishing a link only in vague terms between the Baroque palace façades. In 2007, the design by the Italian architect Franco Stella triumphed

2015

Photo: Jasmine Deng

Photo: Philipp Meuser

in an architectural competition, whereby the latter divided the interior of the palace-cube into three public areas: Schlüterhof (Schlüter Courtyard) – three sides of which have been reconstructed – a central open passage and an entrance hall instead of the original Eosanderhof (Eosander Courtyard). A large-scale grid-like façade facing the Spree is gradually emerging. The ruined palace of Prussian kings and German emperors had its origins in the fortress built as of 1443, with which the Margrave and Elector of Brandenburg sought to monitor the city. The building primarily owes its current popularity to the Baroque conversions and expansions by Andreas Schlüter and Johann Eosander von Göthe which, however, would always remain magnificent fragments of an overall incomplete conception. Neither of them would presumably come up with the idea of restoring the oblique-angled colossus with all its irregularities since it is precisely these which they tried to conceal with every means available, along Baroque lines. All urban shortcomings arise anew from the three palace façades: towards the east, facing the former urban centre beyond the Spree, the palace showcases an inferior façade. To the west, the dome is to be reconstructed in all its previous splendour and one again faces west, into Nothingness, with the loss of all architectural appeal. The palace is misaligned with the Altes Museum (Old Museum) designed by Schinkel. Neither of the two entrances to the Lustgarten (Pleasure Garden) lies, even on an approximate basis, on its central axis. Since 2011, the Humboldt-Box by KSV Krüger Schuberth Vandreike has provided information on the construction project. Malicious gossip has it that the temporary building is to persuade discerning visitors of the lack of aesthetics by contemporary architects and thus win them over for the reconstruction.

2016

Photo: Philipp Meuser

Humboldt-Forum

Elevation Schlossfreiheit

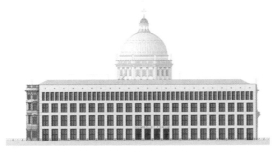

Elevation Spree

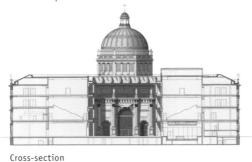

Cross-section

Original floor plan of the second floor

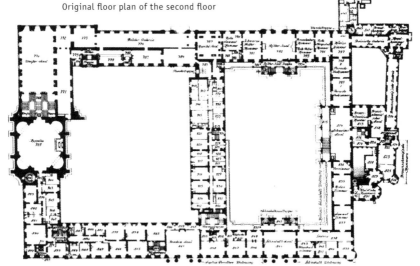

Elevation Lustgarten

Elevation Schlossplatz

Longitudinal section

Intended floor plan of the second storey

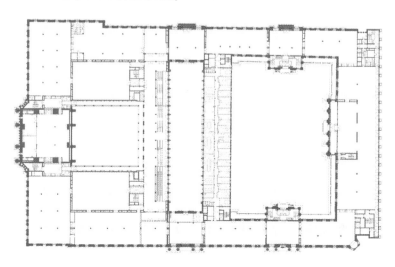

Plans: Stiftung Berliner Schloss – Humboldtforum/Franco Stella

Hidden beneath the dome: the Dom-Museum with
an exceptional collection of architectural models

Photo: Friedrich Albert Schwartz

Berliner Dom

Am Lustgarten
Julius Raschdorff, Günter Stahn
1905, 1981, 1993

A 019

As early as the nineteenth century, the modest preceding building, which was built by Boumann and Knobelsdorff in 1750 and furnished with classical alterations by Schinkel in 1821, was regarded as not stately enough. The construction of a two-tower basilica according to designs by Friedrich August Stüler never extended beyond several foundation walls and was abandoned in 1848. Under the strong influence of Wilhelm II, Julius Raschdorff built the current Berliner Dom (Berlin Cathedral) between 1894 to 1905 with references to Baroque and Renaissance forms. Nothing less than the Protestant counterpart to St. Peter's Basilica was to be constructed – however, contemporaries felt the monumental design vocabulary to be obtrusive and anachronistic. Four satellites surround the main dome, beneath which is located the main room of the sermon church for 2,100 people. The Tauf- und Traukirche (Baptismal and Matrimonial Chapel) falls into line to the south. The Denkmalskirche (Memorial Church)

featuring funerary monuments and empty grandiose coffins of the Hohenzollern family was attached as a northern apse and demolished in 1975 for ideological reasons. Numerous members of the House of Hohenzollern are buried in the crypt. The main dome was burnt down during the war. Its lanterns came crashing down and penetrated into the tomb vault. A stylistic tidy up of the façades richly adorned with sculptural ornamentation, planned as part of the reconstruction effort, was prevented. Once the external construction work was completed, the restoration of the interior continued until 1993. In addition to the Denkmalskirche, the preserved lanterns of the two small side domes were also destroyed. The new simplified main dome has a disastrous effect on the proportions of the overall building. When the dome cross, which was designed by Günter Stahn, and the lantern had to be renovated owing to corrosion damage in 2006, the opportunity to restore the original substantially higher version and thus mitigate the stocky impact of the building was squandered. According to the spokesperson for the cathedral, the unfortunate crown of the dome is the subject of a preservation order.

Section: Berlin und seine Bauten, 1896

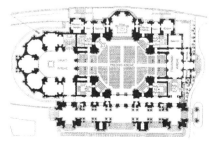

Floor plan: Berlin und seine Bauten, part VI, 1997

Altes Museum
Am Lustgarten
Karl Friedrich Schinkel et al.
1830, 1966

A 020

Friedrich Wilhelm III commissioned the first museum in Berlin to be built between 1823 and 1830 as the nucleus of the Museumsinsel (Museum Island), thus making the royal art collection accessible to the general public. A hall with eighteen Ionic columns is positioned across the entire width on the outside of the rectangular classical building. Behind is the staircase hall connecting both storeys. A glass wall caricatures the flowing transition which Schinkel was seeking to achieve between the interior and exterior space. At its centre stands the Pantheon-inspired rotunda which the exhibition rooms and two adjacent courtyards are clustered around. Only the domed hall was restored to its original state following the war. The remaining interior design and the cycle of frescoes made to Schinkel's designs in the entrance hall have been lost. The courtyards are to be covered and the access redesigned as part of the planned general restoration work by Hilmer & Sattler and Albrecht. The granite bowl in front of the flight of steps was only made from a single large stone and, upon completion, considered to be a wonder of the world. Originally Schinkel wanted to display this in the rotunda. The Lustgarten (Pleasure Garden), which had been demoted to a parade square by the National Socialists, was made into a green space again by Hans Loidl in 1999, whereby he freely interpreted Schinkel's design. Today, the building houses the *Antikensammlung* (Collection of Antiquities) from the Staatliche Museen zu Berlin (Berlin State Museums).

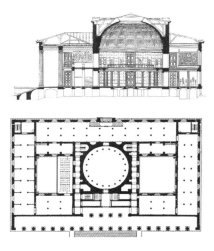

Source: Sammlung Architektonischer Entwürfe, 1858

Photo: istockphoto/mkrberlin

Alte Nationalgalerie

Bodestraße 3
Friedrich August Stüler et al.
1876, 2001

A 021

The banker Johann Heinrich Wagener bequeathed his collection of 262 paintings to the Prussian crown prince, with the request that a museum be built for them. Stüler's design is based on sketches by Friedrich Wilhelm IV which had already proposed a temple-like building flanked by colonnades. After Stüler's death, Johann Heinrich Strack built the Corinthian pseudo-dipteral temple with a projecting open portico and an apse adjoining at the back on the high base. The statue of Friedrich Wilhelm was erected on the landing of an imposing but functionless double flight of steps. Concealed beneath is the driveway for carriages bordering on the vestibule, where the actual entrance is located. Both the exterior and interior architectural ornamentation is geared to the gable inscription *Der deutschen Kunst* (*To German Art*). The two exhibition floors were adjusted several times to meet changing requirements. In 1913, the columned hall intended to exhibit sculptures was split up into several small rooms. In 1935, both two-storey Corinthian halls

at the centre of the building obtained suspended luminous ceilings. The Alte Nationalgalerie (Old National Gallery) was completely renovated as the first building of the Museumsinsel (Museum Island) after the fall of the Wall. Thanks to HG Merz's precautionary approach, the museum's technical fixtures remain hidden from view after the refurbishment. The only small fly in the ointment is the permanent obstruction of the Cornelius halls owing to a false ceiling in lieu of the former suspended one. Two new exhibition rooms for paintings by Casper David Friedrich and Karl Friedrich Schinkel have been built. The idyllic colonnade courtyard was newly created by Levin Monsigny in accordance with the original design. Traditional materials and geometric carpets of vegetation sit unobtrusively behind the architecture and selected sculptures.

Source: Berlin und seine Bauten, 1877

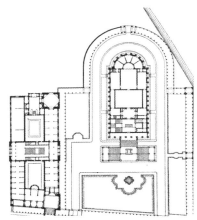

Source: Berlin und seine Bauten, 1896

Neues Museum

Bodestraße 1–3
Friedrich August Stüler,
David Chipperfield Architects
1846, 2009

A 022

The New Museum (Neues Museum) was developed as part of a "sanctuary for art and science" outlined by Friedrich Wilhelm IV. In common with the adjacent Altes Museum (Old Museum), the cubical structure is subdivided into two inner courtyards with a central wing providing access. Stüler's magnum opus impressed his contemporaries with its new industrial design, particularly the partially open iron frame on show. The exhibition rooms were richly furnished in coherence with the exhibited objects – which turned out to be extremely obstructive during subsequent rearrangements of the accruing collections. The Altes Museum, which is lower by one storey, was connected via an arcade. It took more than sixty years

following the war-induced closure until the collections of the Ägyptisches Museum (Egyptian Museum) and the Museum für Vor- und Frühgeschichte (Museum of Pre- and Early History) were able to return to their ancestral home. There had been controversial disputes over the approach to the abandoned ruins pulverised by bombs. David Chipperfield Architects have complemented the original building volume and room sequences in abstract form. This initially won them opposition from a citizens' initiative advocating that it be reconstructed true to the original design. The north-east wing and south dome were walled up by using old brick material. The surviving façades and interior furnishings were conserved and supplemented in small areas only. Dark oak, bronze and fine prefab concrete parts were used for new spatial concepts. Alongside the preserved iron arches, mosaic floors and decorative paintings, one is particularly struck by the restored staircase hall.

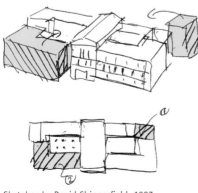

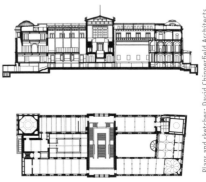

Sketches by David Chipperfield, 1997

Visualisation: David Chipperfield Architects

James-Simon-Galerie
Bodestraße 1–3
David Chipperfield Architects
2017

A 023

In future, the exhibits of the Museums-insel (Museum Island) are to be presented here, covering all the collections at once. An Archäologische Promenade (Archaeological Promenade) will connect four of the five buildings at the height of their base level. A new reception building which is to relieve the historic buildings emerges as a central contact point, particularly for larger groups of tourists. The 1999 award-winning competition project by David Chipperfield Architects encountered fierce criticism. In lieu of the satin-glazed cube there now arises a building somewhat closer to the classical vocabulary of museums. The design restores the urban planning situation prevailing before Schinkel's Packhof administration building was demolished in 1938 and creates an extension to Stüler's colonnades to form the Neues Museum (New Museum). Towards the Kupfergraben, a high base taken over by the Pergamon-museum defines the water's edge. A wide flight of steps points in the direction of the Lustgarten (Pleasure Garden) in the form of a prestigious welcoming gesture and makes the entrance hall accessible. A café and the entrance to the main floor of the Pergamonmuseum – where a short circuit has been set up – are situated within the tall colonnade. Staff areas, special exhibition areas and an auditorium emerge in the base structure. In common with the Neues Museum, artificial stone has been used which is interwoven into the colour spectrum of the Museumsinsel through the use of natural stone components. In naming the building after James Simon, the art collector and patron to whom the Museumsinsel owes several of its most valuable pieces has thus been honoured.

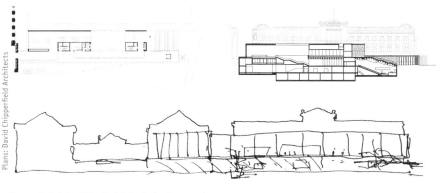

Plans: David Chipperfield Architects

Concept sketch of the Archäologische Promenade

Pergamonmuseum

Am Kupfergraben
Alfred Messel,
Ludwig Hoffmann et al.
1930, 2019

A 024

It was already evident during the construction of the Bode-Museum that further exhibition space was required. The showpiece of the *Antikensammlung* (Collection of Antiquities), in particular, the 113 m long Pergamon Altar, was to be presented in full size. After Alfred Messel passed away a year before construction began, the town surveyor, Ludwig Hoffmann – with whom he was acquainted – implemented his plans in modified form. The last museum on the island was still unfinished when it opened in 1930, delayed by the First World War and subsequent inflation. The collections of antique, Islamic and Near Eastern art were housed in a three-wing complex facing the Kupfergraben. In the shape of ruggedly articulated volumes, Messel focuses on Doric temple motifs, such as those used by Gilly and Langhans around 1800.

The smooth windowless central wing culminates in a terraced structure featuring truncated towers. Flat pilasters lend structure to the side wings. It was not until 1981 that an extension was created for the central reception building. As part of the general restoration work, a fourth wing is intended to border the court of honour in lieu of the unrealised colonnade, thus allowing for a closed circuit within the building. The three collections obtain separate entrances, in keeping with the original concept. Furthermore, a short circuit is envisaged which can be reached from the adjoining James-Simon-Galerie. The exhibition of the architectural fragments from the Vorderasiatisches Museum (Museum of the Ancient Near East), the Museum für Islamische Kunst (Museum of Islamic Art) and the *Antikensammlung* (Collection of Antiquities) will be enhanced by pieces from the Ägyptisches Museum (Egyptian Museum). Jan Kleihues and Walter A. Noebel (†) were commissioned with the execution of the late Oswald Mathias Ungers' designs dating back to 2000.

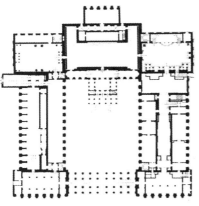

Source: Berlin und seine Bauten, part V, 1983

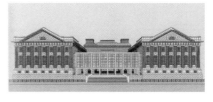

Source: Architekturmuseum TUB

Bode-Museum

Am Kupfergraben
Ernst von Ihne, Heinz Tesar et al.
1904, 2006

The court architect Ernst von Ihne succeeded in creating on the irregular triangle at the tip of the island a building which is seemingly perfect in its symmetry, which houses the collection of sculptures and art works behind its neo-Baroque façades. The rusticated base emerges straight out of the water, followed by two exhibition floors featuring colossal pilasters. The side façades are characterised by four risalits with a tympanum. Owing to their tiered arrangement, the building's presence in the urban environment is enhanced by bridges, the entrance front and the main dome. The prestigious sequence of rooms within the central axis is bordered by the two domed halls, each containing stairs. In between lies a so-called basilica modelled on the church of San Salvatore al Monte in Florence. Altars are displayed in its side chapels. The basic concept of the first museum director Wilhelm von Bode provided for sculptures, paintings and contemporary furnishings to be arranged as atmospheric spaces, so as to broker an overall impression of the epoch. For this purpose, he collected old chimneys, door lintels and furniture, primarily in Italy. The building has borne Bode's name since 1956. For the general

restoration work running up to 2006, Heinz Tesar built a new circulation building in the fifth courtyard and the connection to the Archäologische Promenade (Archaeological Promenade) beneath the small dome. Today, the sculptural collection, the Museum für Byzantinische Kunst (Museum of Byzantine Art) and the *Munzkabinett* (Coin Cabinet) are on display. In future, sculptures and paintings are to be exhibited in correspondence with one another, in accordance with Bode's concept. An extension envisaged on the other side of the Kupfergraben is to facilitate the repatriation of the art gallery from the Kulturforum (Cultural Forum) in West Berlin to the Museumsinsel (Museum Island). Following the decision to first expand the Neue Nationalgalerie (New National Gallery), the plans have, however, been put on the backburner.

A

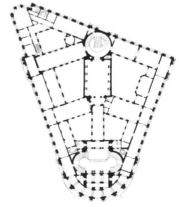

Source: Berlin und seine Bauten, part V, 1983

The Former West:
Kurfürstendamm

Kaiser-Wilhelm-Gedächtniskirche (Egon Eiermann, 1963) and
Upper West (Christoph Langhof, KSP Jürgen Engel Architekten, 2017)

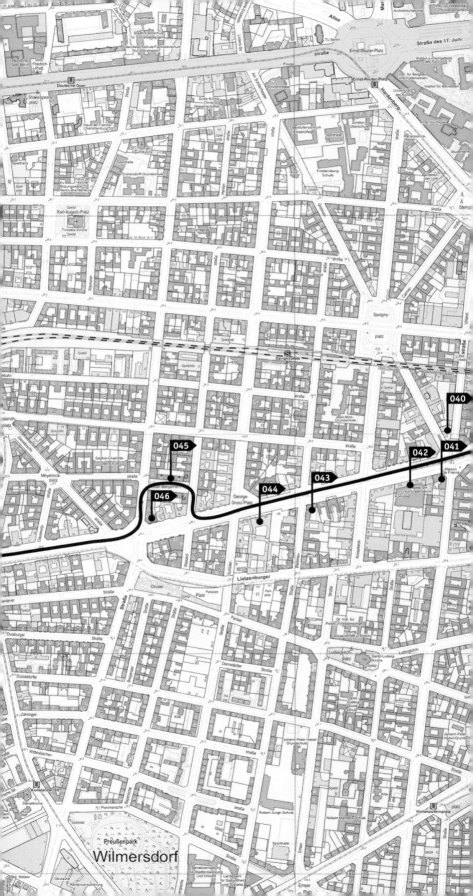

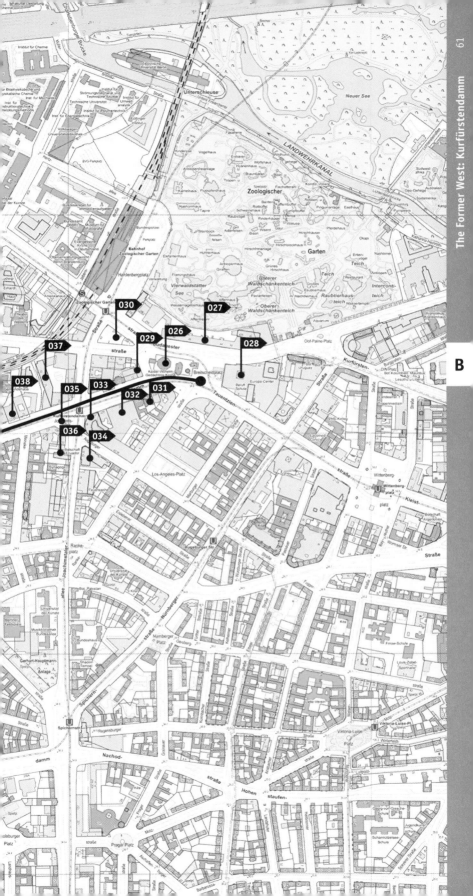

B

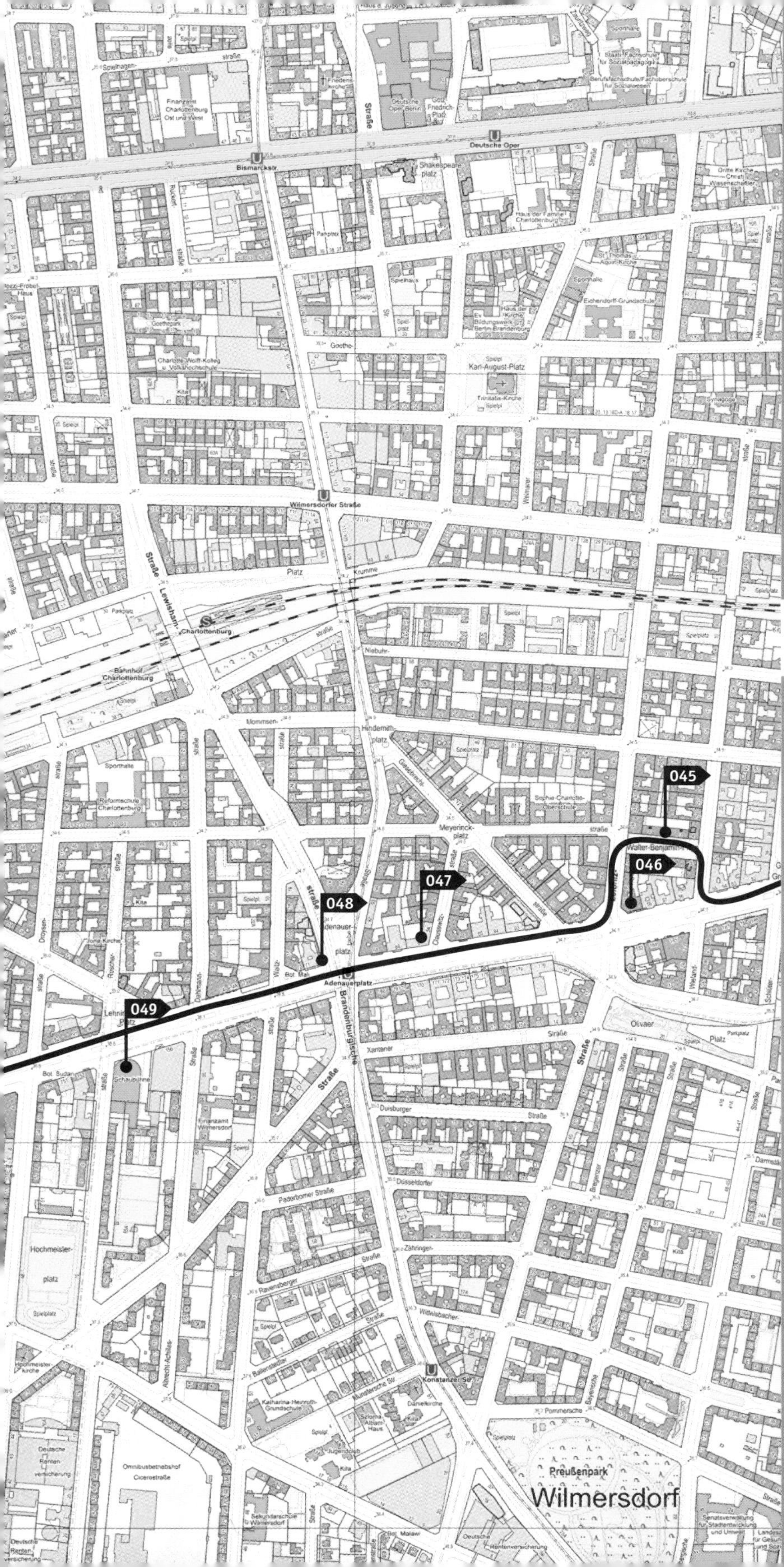
045
046
047
048
049
Deutsche Oper
Bismarckstr.
Shakespeareplatz
Karl-August-Platz
Wilmersdorfer Straße
Charlottenburg
Bahnhof Charlottenburg
Lewisham-Straße
Mommsen-
Niebuhr-
Hindemithplatz
Meyerinckplatz
Sophie-Charlotte-Oberschule
Walter-Benjamin-Platz
Adenauerplatz
Brandenburgische Straße
Lehniner Platz
Schaubühne
Olivaer Platz
Xantener
Duisburger Straße
Düsseldorfer
Paderborner Straße
Zähringer-
Ravensberger
Wittelsbacher-
Konstanzer Str.
Hochmeisterplatz
Preußenpark
Wilmersdorf

2013

030

Zoologischer Garten Station

C/O Berlin Gallery

037

038

Kurfürstendamm with a view of Breitscheidplatz
and Joachimsthaler Platz to the east

Zoologischer Garten Berlin

027

026

028

029

031

032

033

034

036

B

2009

046

0

044

043

042

041

040

039

038

View along Kurfürstendamm and the railway line towards the west

Interior of the old Kaiser-Wilhelm-Gedächtniskirche
with its distinctive ceiling mosaics

Source: Zentralblatt der Bauverwaltung, 1895, No. 13

Photo: iStockphoto/Holger Mette

Kaiser-Wilhelm-Gedächtniskirche

B 026

Breitscheidplatz
Franz Schwechten, 1895
Egon Eiermann, 1963

The symbol of the former West Berlin came about as a compromise. In the wake of vigorous protests, Egon Eiermann was forced to dispense with a complete demolition of the church – which had been severely damaged in the Second World War – as envisaged in the competition design. Instead, the tower stump became the centre of a five-piece ensemble consisting of an octagonal nave and rectangular foyer as well as a hexagonal tower and rectangular parish chapel. Any formal approach to the ruins was avoided. All components are covered with distinctive concrete grid blocks, and the more than 20,000 openings in these were filled with coloured glass shards by Gabriel Loire. The backlit double shell walls transmit the deep blue hue from the sacred to the urban environment in the evening. Eiermann designed all significant interior elements himself, from the altar to the organ prospect. When it came to building the old church, Franz Schwechten opted for the *Rhenish Romanesque* style. Together with stylistically conformist buildings, this formed the captivatingly quirky Romanische Forum (Romanesque Forum) in which the Dark Ages and the up-and-coming metropolis were bonded together. A 113 m high main tower and four lower peripheral towers soared above a Latin cross floor plan. The angled positioning in the road network fully accentuated the prominently tiered components. In addition to its essential function, the church also served as a memorial to the deceased emperor. The mosaics in the vestibule betray the desired legitimacy of the German imperial state by the Grace of God and convey a picture of former splendour.

B

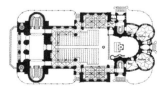

Design by Franz Schwechten, 1895
Source: Berlin und seine Bauten, 1896

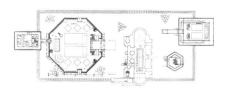

Design by Egon Eiermann, 1963
Source: Berlin und seine Bauten, part VI, 1997

Interior of the new Kaiser-Wilhelm-Gedächtniskirche with its distinctive blue glass walls

B

Source: Bayerische Hausbau, image: Franz Brück

Bikini Berlin, former Zentrum am Zoo

B 027

Budapester Straße 38–50
Paul Schwebes, Hans Schoszberger,
SAQ architects, Maske + Suhren,
Hild und K
1957, 2014

An awakening and faith in the future were manifested after the war in the development of the area around Kaiser-Wilhelm-Gedächtniskirche (Kaiser Wilhelm Memorial Church). Following the Berlin Blockade, the "window display of the West" arose here to which the creation of the Berlin International Film Festival in 1951, the Interbau housing development in 1957 and the miraculous upturn in the economy are closely related. An ensemble comprising five sections formed the elongated listed Zentrum am Zoo (Centre at the Zoo) – subsequently known as Zoobogen (Zoo Arch) – in the midst of the landscape of ruins. The curved ceramic façade of the Zoo Palast (Zoo Palace) cinema and Bikini-Haus (Bikini House) – which used to be horizontally divided by an open-sided storey – followed the large high-rise at the station (also known as DOB-Hochhaus, DOB High-rise). The complex culminates in a small high-rise and a multi-storey car park to the east. Colonnades and subtly differentiated façades lent the freely composed ensemble a buoyant lightness in demonstrative contrast to the architectural conceptions of displaced Nationalism. When it came to the revitalisation and renovation by SAQ architects and the Belgium artist Arne Quinze, which were completed

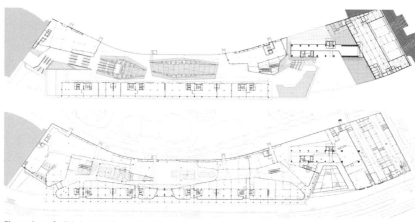

Floor plan of Bikini Berlin following its careful renovation and expansion

Source: Bayerische Hausbau, image: Franz Brück

in April 2014, Bikini-Haus (Bikini House) – the core of the facility – was gutted, expanded and connected with the other sections via a shopping mall joined on to the back. The sculptural free-standing stair towers were forced to give way for this reason. The new shopping centre was given the marketing name Bikini Berlin in the course of rebuilding. The open-sided storey of Bikini-Haus, which gave the building its name and had been closed off as early as 1978, has been given a more open design and is completely glazed. The design for the façade pursues a combination of history and modernity. Projections and recesses with horizontal glass panels give distinction to the surface, with golden elements vertically threaded through it. The so-called Concept Mall in Bikini-Haus spanning three storeys invites one to do some shopping here. A landscaped roof terrace covering 7,000 m² affords a view across Zoologischer Garten (Zoological Garden) and is traversed by trendy indented and projecting features. Beneath it is the two-storey new-build Bikini Berlin Pools showcasing pop-up stores. In addition to shopping areas, the entire building complex contains office premises, catering, places of retreat and a designer hotel in the small high-rise which has also undergone expansion. Maske + Suhren adopted a sensitive approach towards authentically restoring both theatres of Zoo Palast. With a total of seven rooms featuring leather armchairs for 1,650 viewers, the premiere cinema of the Berlinale is once again to emerge as a venue of the International Film Festival.

B

Photo: Zoo Palast

Europa-Center ⌃

Tauentzienstraße 9–12
HPP Hentrich-Petschnigg & Partner
1965

In 1965, the Europa-Center was created as the first American-style shopping centre in the divided Berlin. The high-rise slab measuring 86 m with its widely visible rotating Mercedes star quickly acquired landmark status. The glass and aluminium curtain wall façade was widely emulated. Egon Eiermann, the architect of the Kaiser-Wilhelm-Gedächtniskirche (Kaiser Wilhelm Memorial Church), acted as creative consultant for the construction. Numerous conversions have been carried out over the years. The artificial ice rink thus disappeared, the inner courtyards were covered over and the cinema was forced to give way in order to accommodate the new electronics market. The Weltkugelbrunnen (World Fountain) by Joachim Schmettau, popularly known as the "water-meatball", was inaugurated on Breitscheidplatz (Breitscheid Square) in the year 1983.

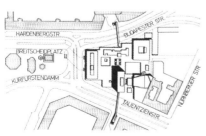

Source: Berlin und seine Bauten, part VIII, 1978

Schimmelpfeng Building

2006

Photo: Philipp Meuser

Upper West B 029

Kurfürstendamm 11
Christoph Langhof,
KSP Jürgen Engel Architekten
2017

Zoofenster B 030

Hardenbergstraße 27/28a
Christoph Mäckler
2013

The idea of both towers on Breitscheid-platz (Breitscheid Square) can be traced back to the Berlin-based architect Christoph Langhof, whose practice was based in the former Schimmelpfeng building (architects: Franz-Heinrich Sobotka and Gustav Müller, 1960). By means of numerous design alternatives, he was finally able to enforce the demolition of this monument in order to free up space for the new development. Langhof had already developed the plans for the resulting high-rise as early as 1995. In common with the neighbouring Zoofenster (Zoo Window), Upper West is to measure 118 m and will also include a hotel and offices over thirty-three storeys. It is scheduled for completion in 2017. A caesura visually divides the sweeping tower – which will soon be among the highest buildings in Berlin – into two slender slabs. Offices and shops are to be built in the base structure featuring a grid-like façade and staggered floors. Langhof is responsible for the urban planning and façade, while KSP Jürgen Engel Architekten were commissioned with the design and project planning. Next door, a pale reflection of the Schimmelpfeng building has survived in the grid-like façade of the former Gloria Palast (Gloria Palace) cinema.

A monument to unloved post-war modernity stood no chance against the euphoria surrounding high-rises in the 1990s. The elegant Schimmelpfeng building, whose bridging wing visually accommodates Breitscheidplatz (Breitscheid Square), was demolished in 1993, althogh it took another decade before a new high-rise was actually built. Christopher Mäckler created two intersecting cubes growing out of a triangular block edge. The refined natural stone façade with windows sitting flush matches the standard of the luxury hotel occupying the most part of the high-rise. The base containing the lower six of thirty-two storeys is guided in its height by the surrounding development. The reference to Gropius' high-rise design for the Chicago Tribune from 1922 is illustrated in the composition of the sections. Due to its location at Zoologischer Garten (Zoological Garden), it was given the name Zoofenster (Zoo Window). The seven-storey glazed crown of the building affords a panoramic view across the capital. Seen from Tauentzienstraße, the intertwining of the ruin with the new building of the Kaiser-Wilhelm-Gedächtniskirche (Kaiser Wilhelm Memorial Church) opposite is unfortunately severely marred by the edifice measuring 118 m.

Marmorhaus B 031

Kurfürstendamm 236
Hugo Pál
1913

Karstadt B 032
Kurfürstendamm 231
Hans Soll, Werner Düttmann et al.
1971, 1983, 1991

Hugo Pál imbued the former cinema with a noble trademark in the shape of the white Silesian marble façade. Four Ionian colossal pilasters lend structure to the façade. Immediately behind the windowless bay – on which hand-painted posters advertised current films – there used to be the silver screen of the large hall. Only three years after a major restoration was carried out (in which the high hipped roof was rebuilt as a glass structure) the UFA announced the closure of the building, one of the oldest cinemas in Berlin. The demise of cinema on Kurfürstendamm has thus continued unabated following the closure of the Gloria Palast (Gloria Palace) and the Filmbühne Wien (Vienna Filmhouse). Nothing remains of the original expressionist interior furnishings featuring paintings by César Klein.

In the year 1971, the Wertheim department store chain opened two new buildings in Berlin. Following the takeover by Karstadt, the name, which is rich in tradition, disappeared from the cityscape in 2009. Werner Düttmann and Hans Soll set back the three lower storeys behind high concrete columns. Five restaurant alcoves level with the first floor floated between them. The side sections and the two projecting upper storeys were composed of narrow bands of windows. In order to adjust the façade to the scale of the street, Haus-Rucker-Co expanded the glass alcoves along its entire height in 1983. The upper edges now form an arc segment. In the year 1991, the stacked storeys disappeared behind a glazed sloping roof with high dormers according to plans by BHPS Architekten.

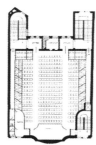

Source: Berliner Architekturwelt, No. 7, 1914

Source: Berlin und seine Bauten, part VIII, 1978

Ku'damm-Eck
Kurfürstendamm 227
gmp Architekten
2001

B 033

Hotel Sofitel
Augsburger Straße 41
Jan Kleihues
2005

B 034

B

For many, Werner Düttmann's Ku'damm-Eck (Ku'damm Corner) from 1972 is synonymous with construction sins committed in West Berlin during the 1970s. The size and cohesiveness of the building were open to certain criticism. With a height of 45 m, the successor building abruptly disrupts the scale of the boulevard. Projections and stacked storeys do not satisfactorily lend structure to the rounded volume. The department store and hotel inherited the foundations and video billboard from the preceding building. The façade is clad in fin-like ceramic parapet panels and aluminium panels. The aim of the sculptural ensemble *Das Urteil des Paris (The Judgement of Paris)* by Markus Lüpertz on the protruding corner was to mediate between the ground plan of the premises and the circular form as well as the traditional eaves' height and the ten storeys.

Quite clearly, the Berlin-based architect Jan Kleihues designed the block tip to graduate in height from 22 m to 61 m and links the heterogeneous solitary Allianz building, Victoria-Areal building complex and Ku'damm-Eck (Ku'damm Corner) to create an overall metropolitan composition. Rounded corners and circumferential parapet panels call to mind both Mendelsohn's Mossehaus (Mosse House) and Fahrenkamp's Shell-Haus (Shell House). Such echoes of modernity merge with the ostensibly classical motifs of the horizontal fluting, the rigorously aligned windows and the symmetry relating to the apex of the building into an innovative whole full of internal dynamism. The physical effect is underlined by the shell-lime façade. Six storeys featuring offices and apartments are located above the hotel.

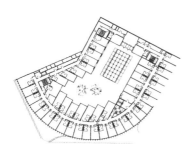

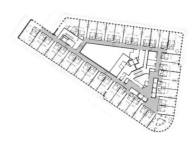

Source: Kleihues + Kleihues and Dülmen-Rorup Archives

Traffic Tower ≪
Joachimstaler Platz
Werner Düttmann, Werner Klenke
1955

B 035

For a mere seven years, traffic lights at the highly frequented intersection were switched on manually according to traffic volume by a police officer sitting at an elevated height of 4.5 m. Since 1962, Berlin's sole remaining traffic tower has been non-operational. The completely glazed "crow's nest" with slightly angled panes and deep blue glass panels is supported by a concrete pylon. It penetrates a filigree concrete roof covering a sales pavilion and an entrance to the metro station. Clocks have been integrated into the front sides of the control desk. The dynamically curved ensemble is a charming piece of everyday architecture from the 1950s.

Allianz Headquarters ↲
Joachimstaler Straße 10–12
Alfred Gunzenhauser et al.
1955

B 036

A high-rise slab, flanking wing and a slender crown expand the junction into a square. The elegant ensemble was jointly built by the winning and runner-up participants in a competition. The penchant for monumental constructions can be traced back to Alfred Gunzenhauser. The windows are structured by colossal pilaster strips and framed by closed wall surfaces. All the façades of the reinforced concrete frame are clad in Jura travertine. Peter Schwebes' influence is discernible in the curved wing building. A filigree roof cantilevers over the protruding shopping zone. Spanning almost 56 m, the building exceeded the height of eaves on Kurfürstendamm for the first time.

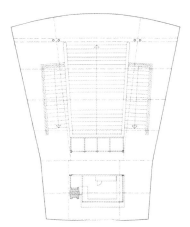

Source: Berlin und seine Bauten, part VIII, 1978

Source: Berlin und seine Bauten, part IX, 1971

Victoria-Areal ⌃
Kurfürstendamm 18/19
Hanns Dustmann, Helmut Jahn
1963, 2001

B 037

Hanns Dustmann, who oversaw reconstruction in Vienna under the National Socialist regime, continued his career after the war. His listed ensemble comprising an office block, a flat row of shops, a rotunda housing a café atop and a windowless department store facing the street marks a caesura in an area covering 22,000 m² within the streetscape of Kurfürstendamm. The edifices clustered around a public courtyard are clad in Roman travertine, complemented by inlays and balustrade areas made of other stone materials. Red window profiles with gold anodising enhance the high-quality materials. The Café Kranzler inherited the red and white awnings, the building's trademark from the pre-war area. The West Berlin institution was, however, shut down in 2000. Today the rotunda houses a smaller café under its former name. In 2001, Helmut Jahn built a tapering 60 m high glazed colossus, namely the Neue Kranzler Eck (New Kranzler Corner), in lieu of the unrealised office slab outlined in the original plans. The light installation by the artist Yann Kersalé enables the building to shine forth in darkness.

B

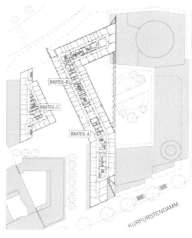

Haus Wien ⋙   B 038
Kurfürstendamm 26
Nentwich & Simon
1913, 1953, 1983, 2013

Kempinski Hotel Bristol ⋘   B 039
Kurfürstendamm 27
Paul Schwebes
1952, 1958, 1967

Prior to the year 2000, the Haus Wien (Vienna House) was home to the Filmbühne Wien (Vienna Filmhouse), one of the first true cinemas in Berlin. The monumental shell-lime façade in minimalist antique-style forms betrays the high regard for the medium. Four colossal Ionian half-columns soar above the base. A closed panel extending the height of one storey has been inserted between the frieze and tympanum. The pitched roof of the lower building unit adjoining one side – where the big main staircase is located – was forced to give way to an uncouth extension. Following many years during which this building stood vacant, an Apple store opened in 2013, the four storeys of which also include the 8 m high cinema hall.

None of the famous hotels survived the Second World War. With its bold sweeping apex set back 6 m from the old alignment of Fasanenstraße, Berlin's first post-war hotel dominates the junction between Kurfürstendamm and Fasanenstraße. The lettering above the corner edifice has no longer been preserved in its original state. The façade is clad in dark-glazed panel on the ground floor and glazed panels shining bright on the upper storeys. Combined with the gold anodised window frames, these anticipate the glossy sheen of the economic boom. A cantilevered café terrace on the roof of the base emphasises the accentuated flexibility of the forms, including its awnings fanning out. The reception hall featuring an elliptical stair is connected to the main entrance to Fasanenstraße. This was accompanied by a seven-storey wing-extension in 1958, followed by a twelve-storey high-rise on the north side in 1967 which is currently threatened with demolition.

Source: Berlin und seine Bauten, part VIII, 1980

Office Building ⩙

B 040

Kurfürstendamm 32
Hans Geber, Otto Risse
1956

Maison de France ⩘

B 041

Kurfürstendamm 211
Wilhelm Klopsch et al.
1897, 1927, 1950

B

In the shape of the concavely curving high-rise, the tapering block acquired a striking apex in 1956 and Kurfürstendamm a square-like expansion. The former administration building of the Hamburg Mannheim Insurance company comprises a ten-storey high-rise with a side wing. The grid façade made of light travertine obtains its three-dimensional effect through the deep-seated windows with recessed balustrades made of green marble. The logo of the insurance company was originally affixed to the left closed façade strip of the building's forefront. A single-storey glazed entrance enhances the asymmetrical tension. In 2015, the listed building was completely renovated. In the wake of this, the entrance area was also redesigned.

The metamorphosis of the corner building is illustrated by the three formative construction phases of Kurfürstendamm and related tendencies in the first half of the twentieth century. In 1927, Klopsch's upper-class dwelling was adapted by Hans and Wassili Luckhardt and Ankerto to conform with the *Neue Sachlichkeit* (New Objectivity) movement. Domes and stucco décor disappeared in favour of a flat rooftop, smooth plaster surfaces and balustrades. Glazed shops were built on the ground floor. In 1950, three flat symmetrical façades (among the most elegant to have arisen from renovations carried out on Kurfürstendamm) came about by removing the oriels and corner windows during the reconstruction as the Institut Français Berlin (French Cultural Institute).

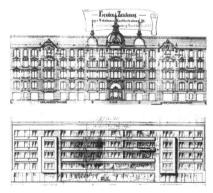

Source: Der Kurfürstendamm, 1986

Ku'damm-Karree

Kurfürstendamm 209
Sigrid Kressmann-Zschach et al.
1974, 2017

B 042

Hidden within the interior of the office and business complex built by Sigrid Kressmann-Zschach in 1972 is not only a gloomy shopping arcade and a twenty-storey high-rise, but the Theater und Komödie am Kurfürstendamm (Theatre and Comedy on Kurfürstendamm). In 1921 the architect of the theatre, Oskar Kaufmann, converted the low, deeply recessed exhibition building into a small boulevard theatre with 798 seats. Prior to 1924, he built a five-storey commercial building with an expressionist façade on the neighbouring plot. For Max Reinhardt he also redesigned the nascent shell of the cinema in the courtyard, to make it into an auditorium. The Komödie is designed as a box theatre with 469 seats. In 1928, Reinhardt also took over the older theatre which was rebuilt by Kaufmann. Both buildings were renovated in simplified terms after the war. They remained unaffected during the construction of the Ku'damm-Karree shopping centre. According to controversial plans by Kleihues + Kleihues, the complex is now set to be converted into an open courtyard opening on to Kurfürstendamm in a manner evoking a square. An auditorium that has been banished underground is intended to take the place of the two historic stages cleared for demolition, since these hinder maximisation of rentable space.

Exhibition house of the *Berliner Sezession*, 1907

Office building, 1924

Komödie am Kurfürstendamm

Theater am Kurfürstendamm

Dwelling and Office Building ≈ B 043
Kurfürstendamm 197/198
Klaus Beyersdorff et al.
1979

Haus Cumberland ≈   B 044
Kurfürstendamm 193/194
Robert Leibnitz
1912, 2013

The seven-storey building on the corner of Bleibtreustraße is the work of Klaus Beyersdorff, Uwe Pompinon and Hasso von Werder. Based on the once obligatory corner cupolas, the tower-like corner of the building projects outward on to the streetscape. Narrow window slits and corner balconies are carved into the predominantly enclosed body. Rounded corners distinguish it from the lower façades which feature full-length windows. Neighbouring buildings adopted the differing heights of the shopping zone. Owing to the numerous projections, recessions and carved openings, the plastered façade evokes housing dating back to the 1920s, such as Hans Scharoun's apartment building on Kaiserdamm.

In 1912, a luxurious "boarding house" with three prestigious inner courtyards was built on an area covering 60 m x 180 m. Robert Leibnitz, the architect of the old Adlon hotel, created smooth plaster façades without historic ornamentation. The view facing Kurfürstendamm is conditioned by a high freestone base and three risalits with angular alcoves and balconies. The business model of suites for rent with domestic staff included failed even prior to the opening. Elegant pieces of furniture were auctioned off on account of the insolvency. The building has housed luxury apartments since 2013, following many years during which it stood vacant. Its name is a reference to Ernst August, the third Duke of Cumberland.

B

Source: Komödie und Theater am Kurfürstendamm, 2007

Source: Berliner Architekturwelt, 1913, No. 10

Ku'damm-Karree with a passage and theatres

Haus Cumberland

Leibniz Kolonnaden ☌

Walter-Benjamin-Platz
Kollhoff / Timmermann
2000

B 045

Dwelling and Office Building »

Kurfürstendamm 59/60
Hans Toebelmann, Henry Gross
1907

B 046

The hitherto undeveloped plot was given over to an elongated city plaza modelled on the Uffizi gallery in Florence. It is flanked by two uniformly designed buildings with colonnades. Only a fountain and a single chestnut tree occupy the ends of the plaza. The minimalist design reinforces the impression of an idealistic design idea dating from the Renaissance. The minimal variation in the façades, however, seems somewhat half-hearted. Made up of dark grey stone slabs, they reflect an abstract classicism. Although fine woods, bronze doorbell panels and mosaic floors complement the noble picture, these stand in contrast to the lower storey heights measuring 2.5 m. Apart from shops, the buildings are home mostly to apartments and office premises. A nursery is located on the roof.

Otto von Bismarck not only enforced the expansion of the royal bridlepath into a 53 m wide boulevard, but also the obligatory corner cupolas. Arguably the most impressive one, which is flanked by two satellites, can be found at the striking building on the corner to Leibnizstraße. The copper roof section was faithfully reconstructed in 1994. Only the sumptuous corner building has preserved its original façade ornamentation out of the four grand residential buildings along Kurfürstendamm. Located on each storey are an upper-class eight-room apartment covering 410 m² and an eleven-room apartment covering 575 m². It took the Olympic Games in 1936 until the front gardens along Kurfürstendamm were disposed of. The fences were usurped by the rows of display windows preserved today.

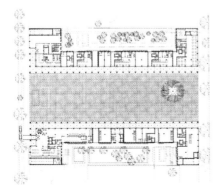

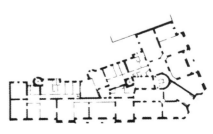

Dorette-Haus ⩣

Kurfürstendamm 67
Heinrich Sobotka, Gustav Müller
1956

B 047

The corner building dating back to 1956 not only seems dynamic owing to the tiering from eight storeys on Kurfürstendamm to six on Clausewitzstraße. Working within the tradition of the *Neues Bauen* (New Building) movement from the 1920s, bands of windows and balustrades lend a horizontal rhythm to the reinforced concrete frame. Separated skylights and the contrast of balustrades in light travertine and ceiling plates made of darker shell limestone further emphasise the horizontal aspect. Only the tower-like projecting risalit with concrete ribs expresses a vertical counterpoint. Contrary to assumptions, the stairway is not located here. The access core is located on the courtyard side. The building owes its name to the garment manufacturer Dorette-Kleider which has only existed for about a decade. The construction of the wall spelt the end for the burgeoning fashion industry in the 1960s on Kurfürstendamm.

B

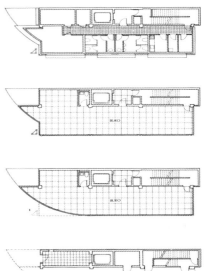

Ku' 70 ≈

Kurfürstendamm 70
Helmut Jahn
1994

Lewishamstraße, which is diagonally intersected by the block structure, is a relic of car-oriented urban planning in the 1960s. Helmut Jahn developed the remaining land covering a mere width of 2.5 m to form Kurfürstendamm, but did not seek to visually bridge the gap. Above the ground floor extending across 60 m², the glass and steel construction sprawls to more than twice the 5.5 m depth of the building. The dynamic curvature endeavours to awaken associations with buildings by Erich Mendelsohn. In common with Kranzler Eck (Kranzler Corner), which was created six years later by Jahn, a tapering glazed corner juts out into Rathenauplatz (Rathenau Square). Here the gesture, however, is somewhat more true-to-scale and compatible. A wide electronic billboard in the upper part clad in lamellae emphasises its technical nature. A 50 m high corner mast bearing the name of the building elongates the oriel-like projection of the façade.

Schaubühne ↳

Kurfürstendamm 153
Erich Mendelsohn et al.
1928, 1981

B 049

Rathenauplatz ↖

Rathenauplatz
Wolf Vostell
1987

B 050

B

The so-called WOGA-Komplex (WOGA Complex) was not only innovative in Berlin owing to its dynamic forms, but also through the combination of dwellings, an apartment hotel, the row of shops, a cabaret and tennis courts. The perimeter block developments continued to be built up to 1927 in accordance with plans by Jürgen Bachmann. Erich Mendelsohn's former Universum cinema juts out into the cityscape with its clinkered semi-circle and the light ventilation chimney as a ship-like entrance hall. Only the sweeping apex of the original edifice remains intact after heavy destruction by war, renovation and a conversion into a playhouse, preceded by major demolition. Curiously, the building had been listed a year beforehand. It is possible to create all classic theatre forms from the proscenium stage to the amphi-theatre in Jürgen Sawade's fully versatile interior space. The hall may be split into three halls, with performances given in concert to one another by means of two rolling shutters.

Rathenauplatz (Rathenau Square) marks the western end of Kurfürstendamm. It firstly emerged in 1958 during the construction of the urban motorway which is routed underneath it through a tunnel. In the year 1922, the eponymous Foreign Minister Walther Rathenau fell victim to an assassination in the adjacent Königsallee. To mark the 750 year anniversary, a boulevard of sculptures extended between Rathenauplatz and Wittenbergplatz (Wittenberg Square). In order to depict the *24-stündige Tanz der Autofahrer ums Goldene Kalb* (*Twenty-Four Dance of Motorists around the Golden Calf*), Wolf Vostell encased two Cadillacs in concrete, and, in doing so, referred to Goya's shocking painting of a naked woman from roughly 1800. The two concrete Cadillacs in the form of naked Maja triggered violent protests. Unknown persons had, in the meantime, assembled a Trabi embedded in concrete with the words: *Einigkeit und Recht auf künstlerische Freiheit* (*Unity and the right to artistic freedom*)!

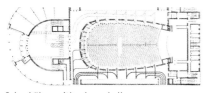

Schaubühne with a large hall
Source: Berlin und seine Bauten, part V, 1983

Schaubühne split into three halls
Source: Berlin und seine Bauten, part V, 1983

On the Trail of the
Berlin Wall

C

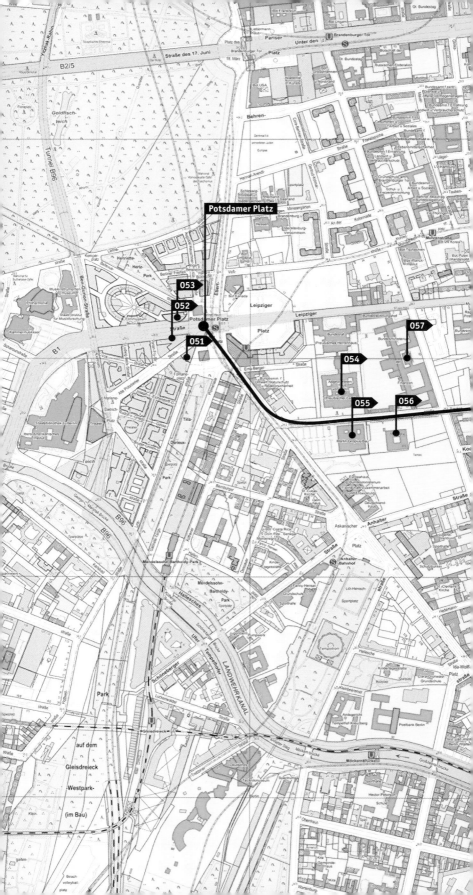

Potsdamer Platz

053

052

Potsdamer Platz

051

057

054

055 056

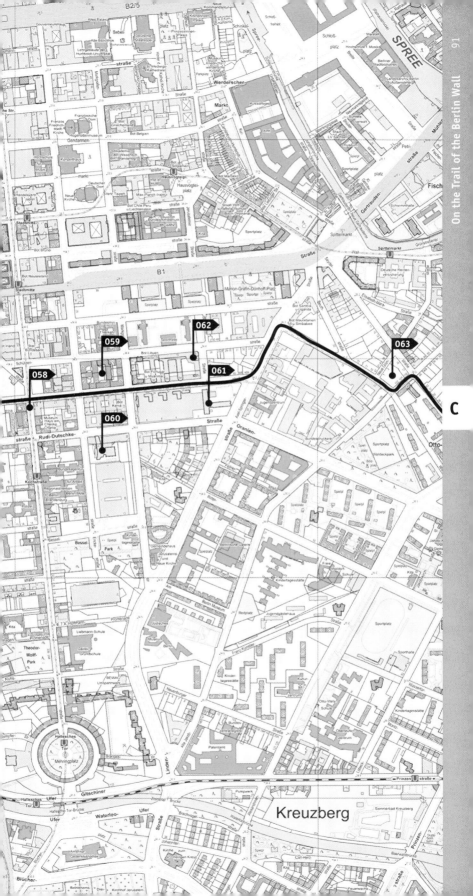

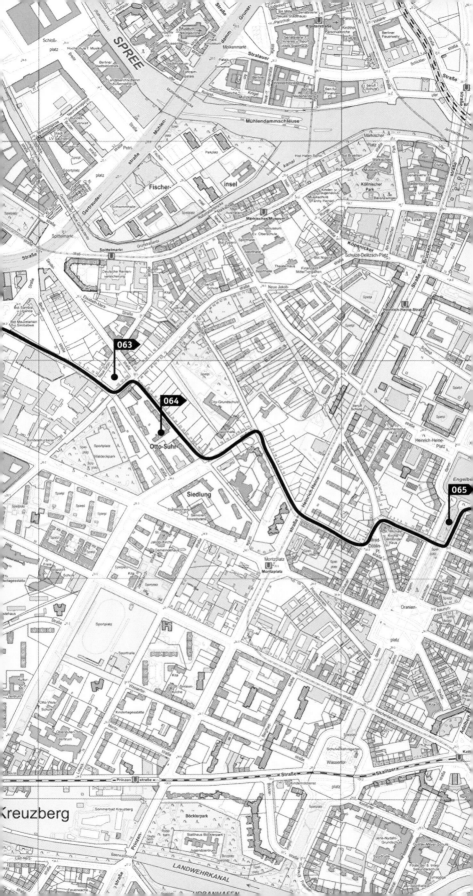

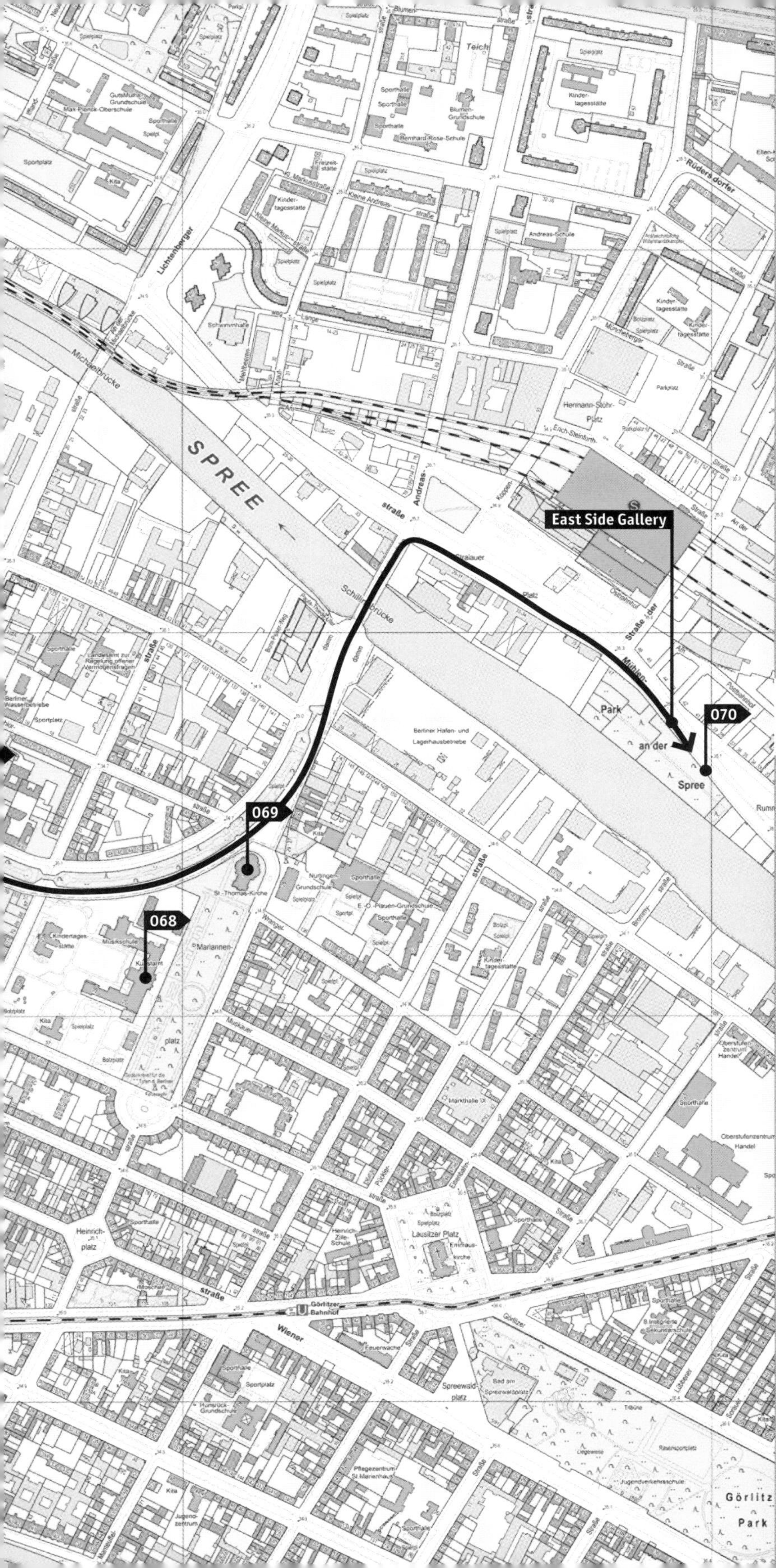
East Side Gallery
068
069
070
SPREE
Schillingbrücke
Michaelbrücke
Lichtenberger
Andreas-
straße
Stralauer
Platz
Mühlen-
Straße der
Park
an der
Spree
Berliner Hafen- und
Lagerhausbetriebe
St.-Thomas-Kirche
Mariannen-
platz
Nürtingen-
Grundschule
E.-O.-Plauen-Grundschule
Markthalle IX
Lausitzer Platz
Emmaus-
kirche
Heinrich-Zille-
Schule
Heinrich-
platz
Görlitzer
Bahnhof
Wiener
Spreewald-
platz
Bad am
Spreewaldplatz
Feuerwache
Hunsrück-
Grundschule
Pflegezentrum
St Marienhaus
Jugendverkehrsschule
Rasensportplatz
Görlitz
Park
Hermann-Stöhr-
Platz
Erich-Steinfurth-
Max-Planck-Oberschule
GutsMuths-
Grundschule
Blumen-
Grundschule
Bernhard-Rose-Schule
Andreas-Schule
Kleine Andreas-
straße
Kl. Markusstraße
Schwimmhalle
Teich
Rüdersdorfer
Müncheberger
Straße
Oberstufenzentrum
Handel
Sporthalle
Kindertagesstätte
Spielplatz
Sportplatz
Kita

A map overlay of urban structures in the city centre in 1940 and 1989
Grey   Pre-war condition of the historic centre (1940)
Red   Post-war condition (1989)
Green Course of the wall (1961–1989)
Source: Senatsverwaltung für Stadtentwicklung und Umweltschutz, Architekturwerkstatt

2008

Holocaust Memorial

053

091

View of Potsdamer and Leipziger Platz

Potsdamer Straße

Potsdamer Platz

Leipziger Platz

Mall of Berlin

Leipziger Straße

C

052

051

2008

060

059

061

062

HÖR ZU   MORGENPOST

Axel Springer Campu

Oranienstraße

Bundesdruckerei

064

View of Berlin-Mitte surrounding Kommandantenstraße

Residential towers on Leipziger Straße

Kommandantenstraße

Beuthstraße

Seydelstraße

C

* according to a design by Rem Koolhaas/OMA

2012

Heinrich-Heine-Straße

Annenstraße

Engelbecken

065

Legiendamm

Leuschnerdamm

View of Kreuzberg featuring the Engelbecken and
neighbouring park in the former Luisenstädtische Kanal

Köpenicker Straße

066

067

C

068

Adalbertstraße

Piano High-rise ⌃
Potsdamer Platz 11
Renzo Piano
1999

C 051

Kollhoff High-rise ⌃
Potsdamer Platz 1
Kollhoff/Timmermann
1999

C 052

In addition to the angular high-rise, Renzo Piano created many other buildings on the site of investor Daimler-Benz. Reddish terracotta tiling unites the Debis tower along the Landwehrkanal (Landwehr Canal), the Arkaden shopping centre on Potsdamer Platz (Potsdam Square) and the musical theatre, among other things. The high-rise measuring about 70 m is clad in a glazed double façade at its peak, which strikes a balance between Kollhoff's perforated façade and Jahn's glazed façade. Behind it is Haus Huth (Huth House) (Conrad Heidenreich, Paul Michel, 1912) which is the sole remaining historic building on the square. The angular tower, oriels and pillars made of shell limestone are a reference to objective tendencies at the beginning of the twentieth century.

American art deco, expressionism championed by Höger and the Märkische brick building tradition are combined in the most predominant building on Potsdamer Platz (Potsdam Square) which became an icon of emerging Berlin after the fall of the Wall. The purple-red clinkered tower ranges from the 35 m eaves height of the rear blocks to 101 m over twenty-five storeys. The lower wings feature a rooftop garden. Resting on colonnades, an extension to the acute-angled floor plan northwards incorporates the theme of a tiered arrangement. The base and window cornices are composed of grey and green granite slabs. As the structure begins to taper with the increase in height, the horizontal emphasis of the balustrades gives way to vertical pilaster strips. The tower is surmounted by a wreath of clinkered struts with golden pinnacles. In common with the Delbrück high-rise at the northern part of the square, Kolhoff and Timermann were guided by American high-rises from the 1920s and 1930s. Hilmer & Sattler and Albrecht created the adjacent Ritz-Carlton hotel along the same lines.

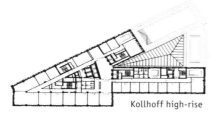
Kollhoff high-rise

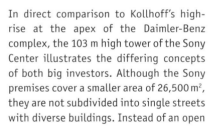

Photo: Philipp Meuser

Bahn High-rise and Sony Center ⇗ ≋

C 053

Potsdamer Platz
Helmut Jahn
2000

In direct comparison to Kollhoff's high-rise at the apex of the Daimler-Benz complex, the 103 m high tower of the Sony Center illustrates the differing concepts of both big investors. Although the Sony premises cover a smaller area of 26,500 m², they are not subdivided into single streets with diverse buildings. Instead of an open urban structure, there arose a large structure comprising several glazed components which are oriented inwardly to the cool oval plaza. This is used as a public place and has connections to the surrounding roads. Fragments of the historic Grand Hotel Esplanade are integrated beneath the striking fanned out tent roof made of panels of fabric. The Bahn high-rise is located at the eastern apex of the triangular building complex and, together with the high-rises designed by Piano and Kollhoff, has become an emblematic feature of the square.

C

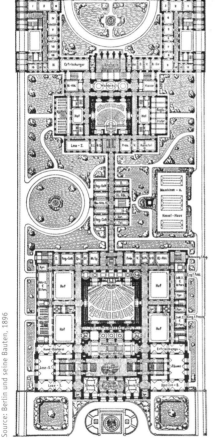

Source: Berlin und seine Bauten, 1896

Abgeordnetenhaus of Berlin

Niederkirchnerstraße 5
Friedrich Schulze, Jan Rave
1899, 1993

C 054

The Herrenhaus (House of Lords) and Abgeordnetenhaus (House of Representatives) jointly formed the Preußischer Landtag (Prussian State Parliament) until 1918. The city planner Friedrich Schulze built plenary buildings connected by a corridor for both chambers on a piece of land which is inserted between two roads. The Preußisches Herrenhaus in the north of Leipziger Straße was completed in 1904 and, following the renovation by Schweger+Partner, now houses the seat of the German Bundesrat (Federal Council). Jan Rave renovated the Abgeordnetenhaus for the Berlin regional parliament and furnished it with a conference room once more. Upon completion, the palatial cube was considered to be a successful functional parliament – particularly in comparison with Wallot's controversial Reichstag (Imperial Diet). Although an Italian-style Renaissance façade with bourgeois connotations made of sandstone was superimposed facing the street, the remaining façades are executed in plaster.

Sources: Album von Berlin, 1900; Album von Berlin, 1900

Martin-Gropius-Bau

Niederkirchnerstraße 7
Martin Gropius, Heino Schmieden
1877

C 055

C

Walter Gropius, who was not otherwise known as an advocate of historic buildings, successfully intervened in 1965 to prevent the demolition of the wartime ruins of the Kunstgewerbemuseum (Museum of Decorative Arts), which is close to the Berlin Wall. The building is named after one of its architects – a great-uncle of the Bauhaus founder – and has provided space for temporary exhibitions since 1981. The palazzo-like cube is regarded as one of the most important buildings of the late *Schinkelschule* (Schinkel school). The brick façade adorned with sandstone elements, terracotta and mosaics is heavily influenced by the Italian Renaissance. The architectural programme makes reference to the exhibits of the building. Since 2000, visitors enter through the main entrance – which was formerly situated in front of the Wall – into the central sequence of spaces comprising the vestibule, atrium and main staircase. The listed building is currently used as a venue for temporary exhibitions and events by the Berliner Festspiele, an umbrella organisation of several festivals which was created in the post-war period.

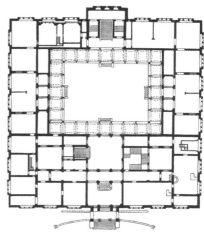

Source: Berlin und seine Bauten, 1896

Topographie des Terrors ⌃

Niederkirchnerstraße 8
Heinle, Wischer und Partner
2010

C 056

The basement walls and foundations of the headquarters of the National Socialist terror regime were not excavated until 1987. The site, which is located next to the wall, was used in part as a driving circuit, and in part as a waste disposal site. Prinz Albrecht Palais on Wilhelmstraße, which was remodelled by Schinkel in 1982, the Kunstgewerbschule ("School of Arts and Crafts") and the Hotel Prinz Albrecht on today's Niederkirchnerstraße were used by the Gestapo, the Sicherheitsdienst (Security Service) of the Schutzstaffel (Protection Squadron, SS) and the Reichssicherheitshauptamt (Reich Security Central Office). After the fall of the Wall, the first competition for a permanent exhibition – which was organised by the Stiftung Topographie des Terrors (Topography of Terror Foundation) – failed to get off the ground. Peter Zumthor won the second competition with a design for an elongated slab comprising filigree concrete stelae with glazed gaps. The proposed bonding method in particular posed major problems. The Land Berlin (Land of Berlin) separated itself from Zumthor in the dispute after the significant increase in construction costs. Three stairtowers costing 13.8 million euros were demolished again in 2004. Following a third competition, Heinle, Wischer und Partner built a functional, solid and neutral exhibition hall on a square floor plan. The central inner courtyard illuminates seminar rooms, the library as well as offices in the cellar.

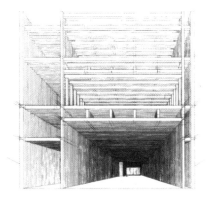

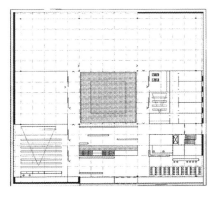

Design by Peter Zumthor and floor plan of the realised building by Heinle, Wischer und Partner

Bundesfinanzministerium ⊻

Wilhelmstraße 97
Ernst Sagebiel
1936

C 057

The National Socialists embarked upon the expansion of the Luftwaffe as early as 1933 in preparation for the war. Ernst Sagebiel, the subsequent architect of Tempelhof Airport, designed the second major building of the regime for the newly created Reichsluftfahrtministerium (Reich Air Ministry). This symmetrical winged edifice encloses two large inner courtyards and a facilities management yard. Sagebiel devised a forecourt at the visitors' reception on the corner leading to Leipziger Straße and a ceremonial courtyard in front of the main entrance on Wilhelmstraße. A reinforced steel frame is concealed behind the smooth shell-lime façade, with sparing use of classicist details. After the war, this centre of power of Hermann Göring, which was left almost intact, was used by the Soviet military administration and then became the Haus der Ministerien (House of Ministries) of the GDR. Today it is home to the Finanzministerium (Ministry of Finance) as the Detlev-Rohwedder-Haus (Detlev Rohwedder House). It is one of the largest building complexes in Berlin with a gross floor space of 112,000 m², 2,100 interior rooms and 6.8 km of corridors.

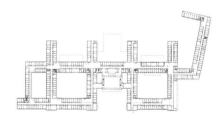

Checkpoint Charlie «
Friedrichstraße 43
1961, 2000

C 058

Quartier Schützenstraße ⌃
Schützenstraße, Markgrafenstraße,
Zimmerstraße, Charlottenstraße
Aldo Rossi, Bellmann & Böhm,
Luca Meda
1998

C 059

C

Soviet and American tanks faced each other here in 1961. Today, the first replica of the control hut on the sector border complete with sandbags and an information sign forms the backdrop for souvenir photos by tourists who visit this place in droves. Actors in Soviet and American uniforms serve as additional decoration. The last functional barracks was dismantled by crane in a formal act of commemoration in 1990, still prior to the German reunification, and brought to the AlliiertenMuseum (Allied Museum) in Dahlem. Far more impressive than the reconstructed barracks is the lightbox which was assembled by the Berlin-based photographer Frank Thiel. This features larger-than-life portraits of a young American and Russian soldier looking into the territory of the former enemy. The pictures were taken in 1994, before the departure of the Allies. Besides Glienicker Brücke (Glienicke Bridge), Checkpoint Charlie is the best-known crossing point in Berlin. It was one of three American checkpoints to be named after the first letters of the international NATO alphabet: Alpha, Bravo and Charlie.

Small plots have hitherto hardly ever been feigned as thoroughly. The restored urban housing block with four inner courtyards on a former wasteland seems to consist of twelve houses. The illusion is betrayed by façades and roof forms repeated at regular intervals, as well as continuous office floors. Concealed behind the brightly coloured façades are offices, shops, a residential building and a hotel. An existing tenancy house on Schützenstraße acquired a façade in an Italian neo-Renaissance style and the base of a house. Aldo Rossi furnished the house at No. 8 with a piece of genuine Renaissance, as a commentary. A replica of the courtyard façade of Michelangelo's Palazzo Farnese adorns its front.

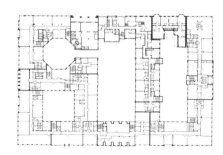

GSW High-rise

Rudi-Dutschke-Straße 22
Sauerbruch Hutton
1961, 1999

As of 1961, the core of the four-piece central administration building of the GSW housing association comprises a high-rise block. Sauerbruch Hutton added as a later extension a slightly concave low-rise building with a dark cladding which restores the original alignment of Rudi-Dutschke-Straße. Towards the east, an elliptical extension clad in gaudy green corrugated metal accentuates the site corner. The slender 85 m tall high-rise slab, corresponding in its orientation to both the Axel Springer high-rise and the residential towers on Leipziger Straße, is highly visible from afar. The tower adjoins the solitary old building at the back. The flying roof on top generates thermal buoyancy to replace stale and heated air between the two glazed façade layers. Sun protection lamellae in various hues of red form the focal design element, lending the building an ever-changing appearance to the west.

Axel Springer High-rise

Axel-Springer-Straße 65
Melchiorre Bega, Gino Franzi et al.
1965, 1994

In 1959, Axel Springer laid the foundation for his publishing house as a political protest against the wind in the former press district, right on the sector border. The Berlin Wall stood a few metres away once the construction work was completed by Melchiorre Bega, Gino Franzi, Franz Heinrich Sobotka and Gustav Müller. The 68 m high tower clad in shimmering gold panels was not only visible from the covered Baroque axis of Jerusalemer Straße, but also from large swaths of East Berlin. The electronic newsreel at the apex has been singled out as a particular nuisance. The construction of the shielding row of high-rises on Leipziger Straße was perceived as a direct response from the East. Gerhard Stössner expanded the tower with a fully glazed wing adjoining it at right angles in 1994. In 2004, a glazed office block by RHWL Architects replaced the listed printing house which offered an aesthetically appealing horizontal counterpart to the high-rise.

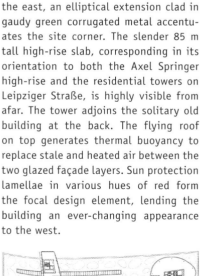

Source: Berlin und seine Bauten, part IX, 1971

Mossehaus

*Schützen-/Jerusalemer Straße
Cremer & Wolffenstein,
Erich Mendelsohn
1903, 1922, 1995*

C 062

In 1903, the architectural practice Cremer & Wolffenstein built a publishing house with an imposing sandstone façade for Rudolf Mosse, the publisher of the *Berliner Tageblatt* newspaper. During the 1919 November Revolution, the exaggerated tower-like corner incurred severe damage through bombardment. Mendelsohn's new, dynamically horizontal corner – together with two extra storeys – became a dramatic counter-image to the outdated prestigious formulae of the Wilhelminian era. Light plaster surfaces with black ceramic bands distinguish themselves in a flamboyant show from the old building and symbolise the dawning of a new era. The corner and the wing on Jerusalemer Straße were destroyed during the war. The building subsequently lay within the restricted zone of the Wall. Reconstruction works were completed in 1995. The abstract street wing in particular, which was refurbished with an additional storey, evokes ambivalent feelings. Today the wing on Schützenstraße is the last relic of the large publishing houses in the former newspaper district.

C

Source: Berliner Architekturwelt No. 7, 1905

Source: Wasmuths Monatshefte für Baukunst, Vol. 8, 1924

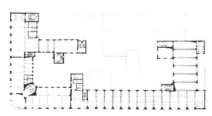

Source: Berlin und seine Bauten, part IX, 1971

Fellini Residences ≋ ≋   C 063

Kommandanten-/Neue Grünstraße
Marc Kocher
2013

The caesura of the former death strip also presents itself in the shadow of the Axel Springer publishing house and slab-like residences dating back to the GDR period. A luxurious or, even better, exotic image is clearly required to sell the apartments at a profit in the no-man's land between Mitte and Kreuzberg.

Forming the current highlights of this development are the Fellini Residences, a three-winged complex featuring seventy apartments of the types Lucca, Venezia and Roma, as well as two underground garage floors. An Italian feeling for life will take a foothold here with cornices, balustrades and pergolas. The architects themselves forthrightly describe their work as the "construction of a striking backdrop". Claudius Seidl (*Frankfurter Allgemeine Zeitung*) sees few Italian features in the design, but rather "that which would have arisen if Baron Haussmann had worked for Erich Honecker, rather than Napoleon III." In fact, the ungainly approach to a historic vocabulary of forms evokes the postmodern phase of the GDR.

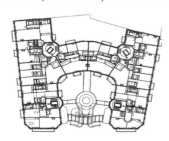

C

Otto-Suhr-Siedlung Project ⩗ C 064

Oranien-, Alexandrinenstraße
Max Rudolph
1963

In 1955, Otto Suhr, the governing mayor of Berlin, declared, "The reconstruction of destroyed urban centres should primarily be fostered at the sector boundaries to counter the impression of stony deserts on the border and express our genuine belief in a future architecture and a new lifestyle compared to the façade culture of the eastern sector". One of the first large-scale construction projects in West Berlin was built in three phases between 1956 and 1963 on the severely damaged area of Luisenstadt. The housing estate defied old road and block structures in favour of a segregation between work and residence – a specific feature of urban planning in the post-war period. The six- to eight-storey rows are oriented towards semi-enclosed courtyards which were accompanied by a fifteen-storey high-rise featuring a number of shops.

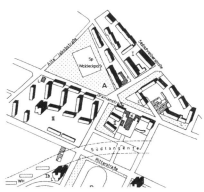

Source: Berlin und seine Bauten, part IV, 1974

Engelbecken – Luisenstädtischer Kanal ⌃

C 065

Peter Joseph Lenné, Erwin Barth
1852, 1932, 2006

Peter Joseph Lenné made the waterway between the Landwehrkanal (Landwehr Canal) and the Spree river the focal design element in his development plan for Luisenstadt. The imposing quaysides were planted with linden trees as part of the city's planned green belt. The canal flowed parallel to the street grid between Urbanhafen and the Engelbecken. The subsequent square bend and the crescent shape towards the Spree stem simply from urban planning. In 1926 the canal was filled in after local communities expressed continuous complaints about smells from the stagnant water. In common with the construction, this was aimed at creating employment.

Erwin Barth, the great social reformist and Berlin-based garden director, resorted to Lenné's idea of creating green spaces near to where people live. He allowed the canal to be filled to the brim, instead of just above water level. A 22 m wide lowered green belt with ten sections of varying design – which can be used by local communities – arose between the quaysides. The water surface of the Engelbecken was preserved – however, an open-air swimming pool planned for it foundered on the protest of the Catholic Church. The green belt was buried beneath rubble after the war. As of 1961, the Berlin Wall cut across it between Waldemarstraße and the Spree. This northern section was excavated following the fall of the Wall and the green space restored in a reduced form. Reconstruction works are yet to materialise south of Oranienplatz (Oranien Square).

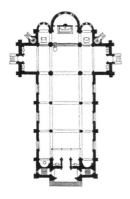

Source: Berlin und seine Bauten, 1896

St. Michael-Kirche ⌃

Michaelkirchplatz
August Soller
1856, 1988

C 066

Deutscher Verkehrsbund ⌄

Engeldamm 70
Bruno und Max Taut
1930, 1951

C 067

C

This Catholic parish church in Berlin is prominently situated within the ensemble of the city as a three-apse brick building with a transept and a high tholobate above the crossing. The figure of the Archangel Michael by August Kiss soars above the turretless front façade featuring a portal niche and a bell storey. August Soller, a pupil of Schinkel, combined his classicist stance with elements of north Italian churches from the Middle Ages and the Renaissance. The transept was restored as a holy place after extensive war damage. A flat parish rectory has been located in the partially open longitudinal building since 1987. The building has now been placed under architectural conservation.

Max Taut executed the Deutscher Verkehrsbund (German Transportation Federation) building according to modified plans by his brother Bruno. He rounded off the corners of the building, designed an additional recessed top floor and implemented the narrow vertical façade grid by means of pillars befitting the reinforced concrete frame. Slender intermediate columns divide the axes into two horizontal window areas each. The main entrance is located beneath a central alcove. The original façade was renovated with dark pillars and parapets in light shell limestone after extensive war damage. In 1978, the foyer was also redesigned.

Künstlerhaus Bethanien
Mariannenplatz 1–3
Theodor Stein
1847

C 068

St. Thomas-Kirche
Mariannenplatz
Friedrich Adler et al.
1869, 1963

C 069

Theodor Stein built the light brick cube of the Diakonnissenkrankenhaus (Deaconess Hospital) according to plans by Ludwig Persius on Köpenicker Feld (Köpenicker Field) which is as yet largely undeveloped. The central chapel at the back is bordered by two side wings. On the main façade a central risalit with pinnacled twin towers and a belfry defines the sacred space and dominates Mariannenplatz (Marianne Square). Over time the main edifice has been extended with numerous outbuildings to form a park-like hospital complex. Of special note are the buildings created by Carl Mohr and Paul Weidner in 1929 and 1930. After its closure in 1970, a citizen initiative prevented the demolition of the main building which is where the Berlin Senate commissioned Künstlerhaus Bethanien (Artists' Residence Bethanien) to be built. Today, twenty-five social and cultural facilities are located on the site.

Once Berlin's largest church, the building flanks the arch of the passage and constitutes the main element of Mariannenplatz (Marianne Square), highly effective in terms of urban planning. Its striking silhouette showcases a blend of romantic elements with Schinkel-style forms and materials. A cylindrical extension featuring a low roof cone and slender spire soars above the crossing. The façade overlooking Mariannenplatz is dominated by a high twin towered complex. Reddish bricks and terracotta make reference to the Bauakademie (Building Academy). When it came to the reconstruction, Werner Retzlaff and Ludolf von Walthausen restored the exterior true to the original design. In the interior, they moved the altar into the centre of the church beneath the crossing. The apse was rebuilt for the organ and choir, while the galleries of the side apses disappeared.

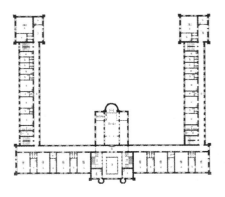

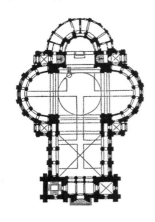

Source: Berlin und seine Bauten, 1896

East Side Gallery

Mühlenstraße 45–80
1961, 1990
Dmitri V. Vrubel (artist) et al.

C 070

C

After the merger of the two German artists' associations, the stretch of wall between Ostbahnhof and Oberbaumbrücke was painted as the first joint project by 118 artists from twenty-one countries. The East Side Gallery was founded upon authorisation by the GDR Council of Ministers. However, a planned travelling exhibition of the Wall segments never materialised. As early as the year 1990, the longest piece of the Wall remaining – boasting a length of 1,316 m – was placed under a preservation order. Known as the *Hinterlandmauer* (inner wall), this blocked off the border strip to East Berlin. The banks of the river Spree opposite in Kreuzberg represent the actual borderline. Following a concrete rehabilitation, eighty-seven of the 118 artists painted their pictures again. There was an outcry among several artists against plagiarisms of their own works, so that today there are gaping white spaces on the longest open-air gallery in the world. In the meantime, two holes were also knocked in the Wall: in 2006, a 40 m wide opening was created in order to connect the newly built 02 World to the Spree and protests of long duration also took place in 2013, when other segments were removed elsewhere in order to restore access to the construction site of a residential tower in the death strip. The investor was, however, committed to investing in the passage. This would lead to the restoration of the Brommybrücke (Brommy Bridge), a pedestrian bridge crossing the Spree which had been destroyed in the war.

On the Trail of
Plattenbau

Ernst-Thälmann-Park, Ella-Kay-Straße 48 (urban planners: Ehrhardt Gißke, Eugen Schröter, architects: Helmut Stingl, Dietrich Kabisch, Marianne Battke, Dorothea Krause et al.)

D

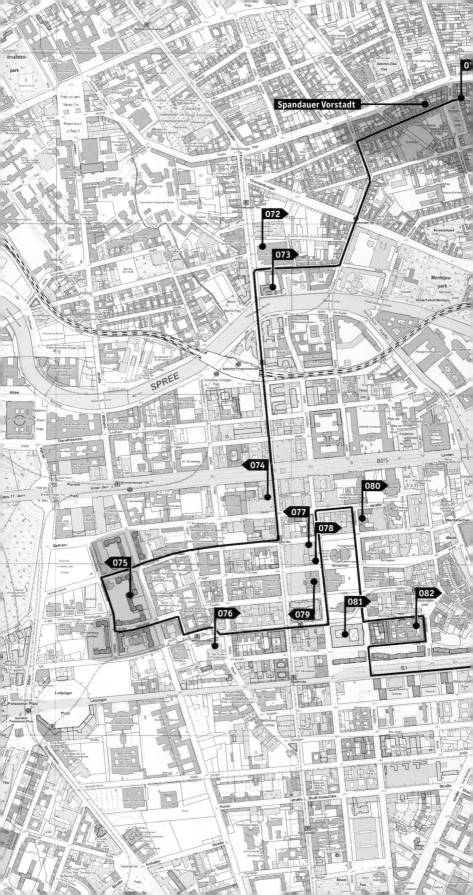

Spandauer Vorstadt

D

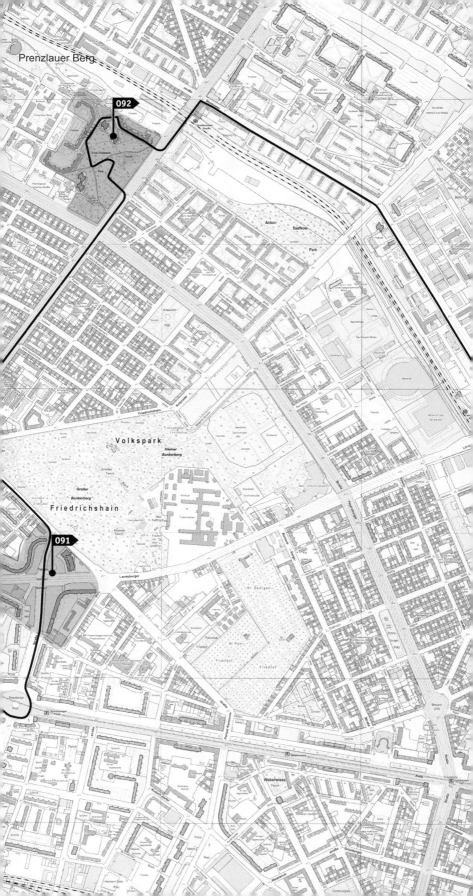

Prenzlauer Berg

092

Volkspark

Friedrichshain

091

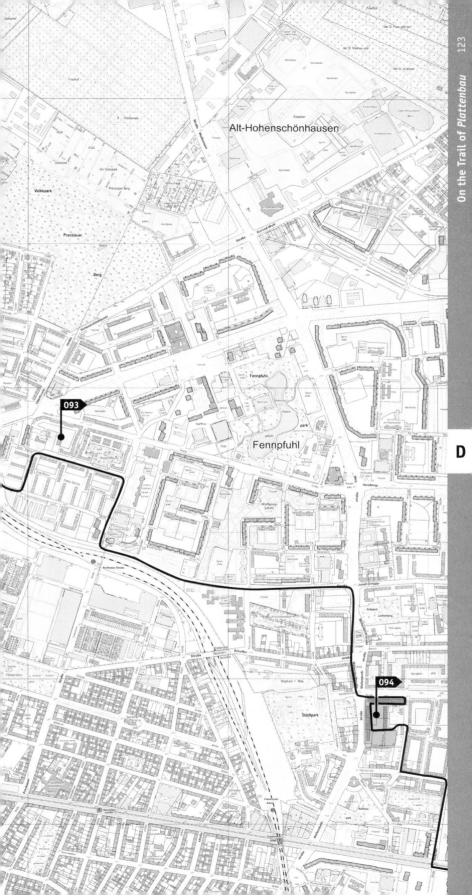

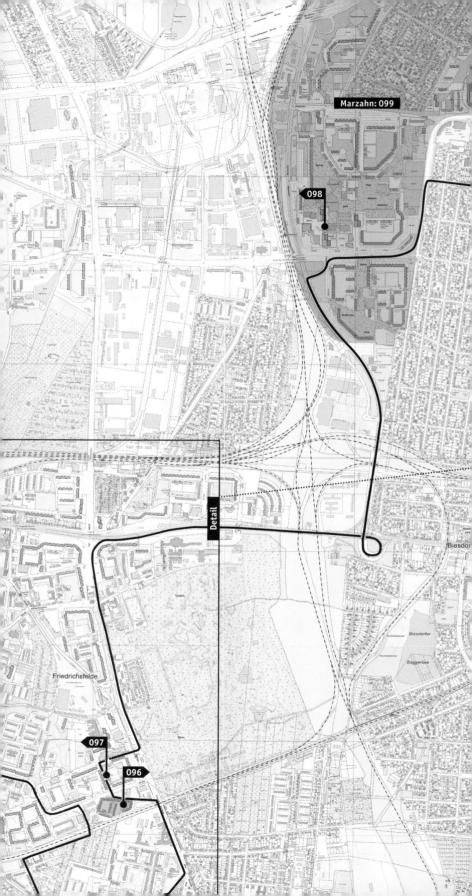

Marzahn: 099

098

Detail

Biesdorf

Biesdorfer
Baggersee

Friedrichsfelde

097

096

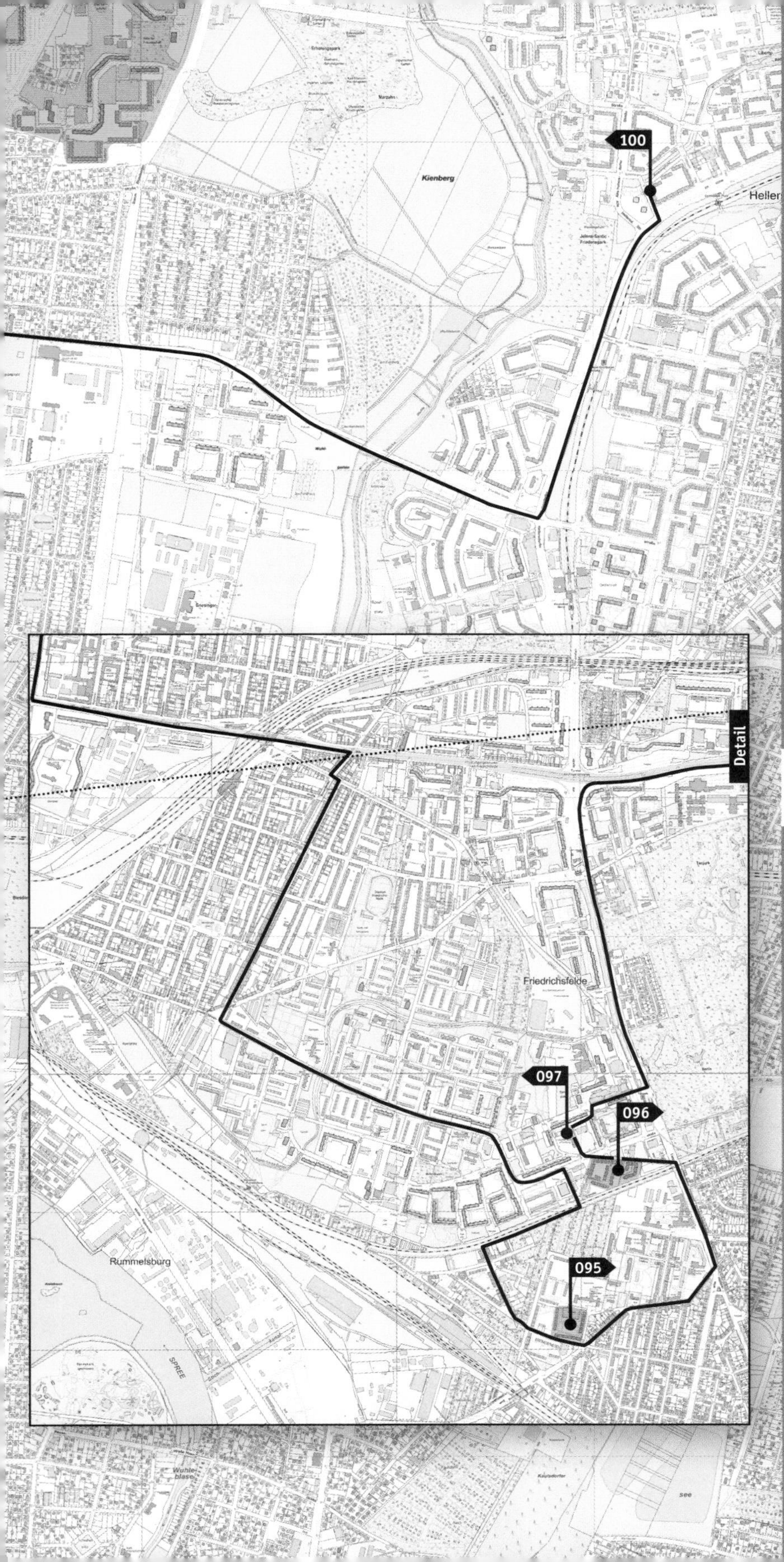
100
Kienberg
Heller
Detail
Friedrichsfelde
097
096
095
Rummelsburg
SPREE

071

072

073

074

Prefab architecture in the district of Mitte

2014

071

089

08

086

083

Prefab architecture in the old city centre

091

090

087

085

084

2014

Ernst-Thälmann-Park and its surroundings

091

Prenzlauer Berg (top left), Fennpfuhl (top right) and Lichtenberg (front right)

2014

095

Karlshorst (left) and Friedrichsfelde (right)

Marzahn: 099

098

Marzahn and Hellersdorf (top right)

Residential building from series QP59 on Karl-Marx-Allee (1 May 1985)

An Excursion into the History of Industrial Construction in the GDR

Philipp Meuser

Industrial mass housing in the GDR has been shaped by two significant political events which mark both its beginning and its end. The first of these was the First Construction Conference of the GDR which took place between 3–6 April 1955 within the Deutsche Sporthalle (German Sports Hall) in East Berlin and stipulated that industrial construction in the GDR was a prerequisite for the advancement of the house-building sector in the GDR. The construction conference in Berlin took place six months subsequent to the All-Union Congress held in Moscow. It was here that a complete restructuring of the Soviet construction industry was established upon the basis of industrial production methods.

The other political milestone is the housing construction programme of the GDR which was decided upon during the tenth plenum of the Central Committee of the SED on 2 October 1973. The politically ambitious objective was to solve the housing question and supply each GDR citizen with their very own apartment. The drive to find a "solution to the housing question within the framework of a social problem" can be traced back to Friedrich Engels, who first formulated precisely those demands (namely, to provide the population with adequate housing) in his contributions for the newspaper *Der Volksstaat* 100 years ago. While the first event held in 1955 had a structural dimension and marked the beginning of first-generation industrial mass housing, the enactment in 1973 was of a political nature. It nonetheless had an impact on construction output: housing series 70 (WBS 70), which had previously been tested and approved for mass production, was regarded henceforth as a remedy leading to the fulfilment of the housing construction programme.

Poster to mark the thirty-fifth anniversary of the German Democratic Republic (1984), design: Klaus Bensdorf

D

Three generations of standard designs for multi-storey mass housing in the GDR can be identified. These generations correspond in essence to three construction methods (block/strip up to load level 2.0 kN, panel up to load level 5.0 kN and panel up to load level 6.3 kN), but are also characterised by other factors, such as transport facilities and urban planning parameters. When setting the load level, the dimensions of the largest component depended somewhat on the availability of transport and the assembly cranes on hand on the construction site. In terms of urban planning parameters, a division according to generations is reduced to the smallest unit which is an entire building for the first generation, a section for the second generation and an apartment or a cluster of apartments for the third generation. Their designs can still be discerned in the city to this day. The first generation witnessed a shift from

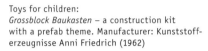

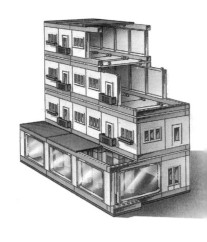

Toys for children:
Grossblock Baukasten – a construction kit
with a prefab theme. Manufacturer: Kunststoff-
erzeugnisse Anni Friedrich (1962)

Nationale Tradition (National Tradition) to the modernity of the East, with rows of housing forming neighbourly residential courtyards. As of 1956, the traditional masonry residential complexes in neo-classical style were complemented by residential buildings from series L4 in large-block construction in Stalinstadt (Einhüttenstadt since 1961), the "first socialist city of the GDR". This attempt to create largely enclosed courtyards with rows of housing is also seen in the urban design concept behind Hoyerswerda, the "second socialist city of the GDR".

The urban construction topography of abstract spatial patterns and geometric patterns were dispensed with for the second generation of mass housing. For example, the site plan for residential complex No. 2 located in the Rostock district of Lütten-Klein follows the pattern of an industrial plant in which both residential and public buildings are lined up like machinery most effectively. In common with the residential estate from the second construction phase on Karl-Marx-Allee in Berlin, the rail system of the assembly cranes influenced the scale of the urban design concept. The distance between buildings spanning up to ten storeys from series QP was calculated in such a way that an assembly crane could serve as many buildings as possible at the same time. Prefab construction was also a characteristic

feature of second-generation mass housing, thus enabling a completely scaffold-free assembly and considerable reduction in the time needed for construction. Regional house-building factories nevertheless developed their own standardised designs, so that the idea proposing a uniform country-wide catalogue of elements could only be implemented to a very limited extent.

It was not until series WBS 70 that the GDR introduced a modular system, achieving maximum individuality in applied architecture upon the basis of a standardised grid and specified basic elements. Urban characteristics on a large scale involved angular building forms in newly constructed residential areas and, on a smaller scale, inner-city developments. This made possible a new understanding of prefab elements. Neither the entire building (first generation), nor a section (second generation) represented the smallest standardised unit, but rather a functional unit, or an apartment, which was able to create any form of building using complementary trapezoidal floor plans. Although housing series 70 is the most flexible system to have been developed in the GDR, it led to monotonous results in most locations. Designers failed to fully exploit the potential offered by WBS 70 owing to the costs and the time constraints involved, as well as political demands for large production quotas.

Toys for grown-ups:
Plattenbauquartett – a quartets-type
card game with a prefab theme.
Cornelius Mangold et al. (2001)

Series L (first generation)

Series L was based on standard designs which had been drawn up as prototypes of type 503 by Hanns Hopp as of 1950. Under the leadership of Hans Schmidt, the Institut für Typung (Institute of Typification) developed, among other things, series L1 (*traditioneller Wohnungsbau*, traditional mass housing/TW brickwork) and L4 (*industrieller Wohnungsbau*, industrial mass housing/IW: large block) as a longitudinal-wall system encompassing load-bearing exterior walls with a load-bearing central wall (each comprising two layers) between which spanned the ceiling. The individual large blocks (L4) were made of either lightweight concrete, brick or vertically perforated bricks and were moved with the use of a crane. The assembled components then had to be plastered. Transverse walls were only 7 cm thick in some cases, made of concrete or vertically perforated bricks and arranged so as to divide up the space. Housing developments could be built as two- to four-storey variants featuring two to four apartments per storey. The brick chimneys of single stoves (coal/gas) protrude out of the 75° pitched gabled roof constructed from reinforced concrete rafters. One main feature was that apartments in residential blocks A to D of up to five segments each were executed in the same size. Only residential block E –

featuring one-, 1.5- and 2.5-room apartments – complemented the choice. However, two- and 2.5-room apartments set the standard.

Series Q (first generation)

As early as 1956, the central Institut für Typung succeeded with series Q in developing a standard design that could be modified by architects at regional level. Hereinafter, variants Q 3a, Q 6 und Q x (type Dresden) proved their worth.

Poster to mark the thirtieth anniversary of the German Democratic Republic (1979), design: Bertold Lindner

Toys for the powerful: the Soviet President and Party Leader Nikita Khrushchev visits a construction fair in East Berlin (1957)

Series Q involved a transverse-wall system which prevailed over the longitudinal-wall system. Hans Schmidt noted that a standard design elaborated for industrial mass housing in Berlin with axial dimensions of 360 cm and 240 cm at a building depth of 2 cm x 500 cm yielded very economical floor plans in transverse-wall construction. Standard design Q 3 succeeded in creating a 2.5 room apartment over an area previously featuring a two-room apartment. It also adopted a two-room apartment with two additional half-rooms within the space of a former three-room apartment, now possessing the dwelling value of a four-room apartment. Variant Q 3a (stove heating) was used in Berlin, instead of variant Q 3 (central heating). Other variants include Q 6 (strip construction) and Q x. The latter was only realised in southern GDR districts and Berlin. The kitchen and bathroom each had a window. Buildings were designed with two apartments per storey to provide for cross-ventilation

Series P (second generation)

Even if standard design Q 3a was built of prefab concrete panels as an experiment and, for the first time, the new construction method also found itself designated with serial numbers with series Q P and P 1, it was not until standard design P 2

that the new generation of industrial mass housing was designed, featuring visible surfaces of wall and ceiling elements made from architectural concrete. VEB Typenprojektierung (State-owned company for the design of industrialised building types) of the Bauakademie (Building Academy) was responsible for centralised handling of the development. Housing series P 2 can be traced back to a design by the collective comprising Wilfried Stallknecht, Herbert Kuschy and Achim Felz which had been commissioned to draw up a standard design on the basis of the existing catalogue of elements, with shorter assembly times and greater profitability. For the first time, an axial dimension of 6.00 m was possible thanks to pre-stressed ceilings. The front length per dwelling decreased from 7.20 m (P 1) to 6.00 m (P 2) for the benefit of a greater building depth of 11.40 m. However, interior design primarily played a part in the success story of this standard design. Although the kitchen had no windows, it did have a hatch opening on to the living room with a dining area which at first met with a positive reception at the *Neues Leben – Neues Wohnen* (*New Living – New Dwelling*) exhibition, where it was displayed in the prototype at Berlin-Fennpfuhl in 1962. In 1959, the Josef Kaiser collective realised, among other things, ten-storey prefab concrete

Industrial prefabrication of large panels in the 1970s

D

slab housing as a transverse-wall system with an axial dimension of 3.60 m within the development of the second phase of the Karl-Marx-Allee boulevard in Berlin. Standard design QP represented an evolution in four-storey mass housing in Berlin. According to official permits, it bore the additional designations 59, 61, 64 and 71. Having been declared a reuse project, it was also realised in other GDR districts. "Development began with QP 59 featuring three apartments per storey, including two two-room and one three-room apartments. Symbolic of the floor plan layout of series QP 71 is the layout of the exterior bathroom and WC, whereby an interior bathroom and WC continued to be designed in independent lodger flats." In common with series P 2, apartments had built-in cupboards in both the kitchen and the corridor to optimise the interior space. This first building type in industrial large-block construction was characterised by a cladding system incorporating colourful tiles as well as the first central heating with its non-adjustable one-pipe circulation. The series was further refined over the years. Although, for example, the balconies on Karl-Marx-Allee in Berlin (QP 59) were fitted at the front of the façade, these were integrated into the building as loggias for a ten-storey building in the Stadtpark (City Park) of Dessau (QP 64). One variant realised in Magdeburg from QP 64 bore the local names M 8 (eight-storey) in addition to M 10 (ten-storey).

Housing series 70 (third generation)

No other standard design for GDR mass housing is so closely associated with politics as WBS 70. On the one hand, it stands for the fulfilment of an ambitious mass housing programme in terms of quantity and, on the other hand, for creative commitment to architectural quality. Although it set out with the aim of counteracting the monotony – repeatedly discussed among architectural circles since the introduction of radical standardisation – with a diverse and extensive modular system, WBS 70 proceeded to become a disaster with regard to East German architectural design. To date, its name is associated

with the lowest point of the socialist construction industry, since – to put it in a nutshell – "the pragmatic house-building factories never actually managed to meet the demands of the supply catalogue". Yet even the greatest advocates of the modernity of the East would be forced to admit that the most inconsequential residential buildings found between Rügen and the Vogtland region were built on the basis of the index cards of standard design WBS 70.

As in series P 2, Wilfried Stallknecht and Achim Felz played a major role in developing the new standard design. On a grid dimension of 6 m x 6 m (floor span length x building depth), the duo designed an even more economical series from 1969 with a view to an overall approach intended not only for use in mass housing. This was laid down in an enactment during the fifth construction conference of the CC of the SED and of the Council of Ministers of the GDR in 1970: the *Einheitssystem Bau* (Unitary System of Construction) now set the direction for house-building factories in the GDR. In addition to the modular system which, in common with a game of Tetris, allows separate apartments as functional units to merge into an overall complex, WBS 70 not only provided a wide range of applications in theory. Local adjustments were undertaken in all districts and documented in the form of complementary serial designations, such as, for example, WBR 83/5 (Rostock), WBR S 84 (Suhl) or WBR Erfurt. Particularly elaborate refinements arose in Gendarmenmarkt (Gendarmen Market Square) in Berlin, where façades were adorned with postmodern ornamentation or mosaics. However, mass housing in the GDR was increasingly dictated by cost savings and fulfilment of a plan. "With each housing construction project, economic proof had to be furnished," recalls former Chief Architect of East Berlin Roland Korn, while Bruno Flierl criticised the fact that, "architects were colonised by economists. They did not build spaces, but were forced to plan the most cost-effective sequence of operations on site." The range of housing built within the WBS 70 system is therefore particularly broad in qualitative terms.

D

Series QP71/10 with striped exterior wall panels at Rosenfelder Ring (Lichtenberg)

Spandauer Vorstadt

D 071

Rosenthaler Straße: execution of the Schwerin district (1985–1987); Torstraße: Iris Grund, Manfred Hartung, execution of the Neubrandenburg district (1984–1988); Große Hamburger Straße: Leichte Platte Cottbus (Light Panel Cottbus) acc. to Hansgeorg Richter, execution of the Cottbus district (ca. 1986); Koppenplatz: Martin Navratil, execution of the Gera district (1985)

Achieving much with just a few resources: following the ban on demolition in central Berlin in 1978 and the first renovations of old edifices, prefab buildings conforming to the old town were built in locations such as Sophienstraße. Additional elements were developed on the basis of WBS 70 in order to build in gaps or curvatures. In terms of roofs, conventional roofing shingles (the extension of penthouses on Koppenplatz (Koppen Square) in the 1990s) or externally supporting concrete panels designed for mansard roofs (Große Hamburger Straße) were used. Similarly, there arose special solutions for oriels and French windows; ground floors were generally allocated shop space, and even the bevelled Berliner Ecke (Berlin Corner) as well as concrete and ceramic ornamentation alike permeated to allow the new buildings to blend in with the old streetscape. Some buildings acquired old wooden doors from demolished buildings (top left: Linienstraße 88). Long, more modern façades were visually segmented into individual buildings (such as Torstraße near Tucholskystraße). By contrast, a more conventional design for WBS 70 with less façade ornamentation was built on Joachimstraße (bottom right). Roughly 780 prefab apartments emerged between 1983 and 1989 in Spandauer Vorstadt. Save for four building ensembles, all have been preserved in their original state.

Friedrichstadt-Palast

Friedrichstraße 107
Walter Schwarz, Manfred Prasser,
Dieter Bankert
1984

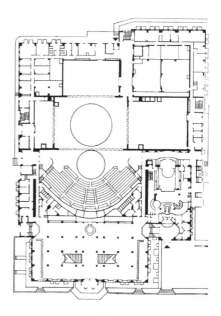

This rectangular edifice was conceived as a revue theatre, a use which it still serves today. The building is a postmodern interpretation of the art nouveau movement: prefab concrete elements featuring heavy ornamentation which imitate sandstone lend structure to the whole façade. The main portal is three-storey glazed oriel, while the steps in front were created in 2011. The huge arched windows of the reception hall are shown to advantage with their colourful glass, evoking stained glass windows, especially at night. In addition, reliefs adorn the ground floor on the north and south side. The foyer is designed as a vestibule with stairs and galleries, glass chandeliers and contemporary stuccowork. Friedrichstadt Palast has the largest theatre stage in the world covering 2,854 m². The administration, technical centre and rehearsal rooms are located within the eastern part of the building.

A special feature is the extendable pool which is located under the stage. The auditorium was designed as an amphitheatre with 1,895 seats, while located to the south is a smaller theatre with a capacity of 240. The building on Friedrichstraße is without a doubt the pinnacle of GDR neo-historicism.

D

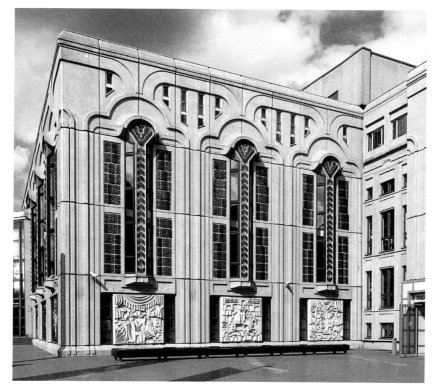

Spreeterrassen Complex « ⌃   D 073
Friedrichstraße 105
Karl-Ernst Swora, Gunter Derdau,
Dera Immaschmied
1987

What a view is afforded by the loggias, oriels and roof terraces of many of the 118 apartments overlooking the Spree and the Museumsinsel (Museum Island)! An experimental unit of the building type WBS 70 featuring extraordinarily sophisticated façades and windows made of anodised aluminium was also built here as part of the new neo-historic Friedrichstraße. The ground and first floors are designed in a monolithic fashion and accommodate hotel rooms and restaurants.

(The Westin) Grand Hotel ⌄   D 074
Friedrichstraße 158–164
Takeshi Inoue / Kajima Corp.
Coordinator: Ehrhardt Gißke
1987

The hotel involves a frame construction with curtain-wall concrete panels. The corner towards Behrenstraße boasts a particularly grand design with a set back top floor and sweeping rows of balconies. In 1985, the northern corner building Unter den Linden – a serial building with a central corridor dating back to 1964 – was given a neo-historic cladding and integrated as part of the hotel. The peculiarity of this is that the building was originally conceived as the Hotel Adlon.

D

Photos: Philipp Meuser

Housing Estate on the Former Otto-Grotewohl-Straße

D 075

Wilhelmstraße et al.
Helmut Stingl
1986–1990

The return to the traditional European city also reached a stretch of the Berlin Wall. Special developments in the prefab building type WBS 70 gave rise to a residential estate with striking façades that replaced Hitler's Reichkanzlei (Reich Chancellery) in direct proximity to Potsdamder Platz (Potsdam Square). Building parts dart rhythmically up and down and back and forth to achieve a sense of fragmentation. Corners arising at the interfaces form an angle of 135° which its windows also follow. Window solutions are customised and include frames using various colours and materials, French windows or oriels, glazed hallways – some of which are fully glazed – and tapering windows on the last floor. Further design elements have corrugated concrete in various colours or recessed loggias with balustrades made of pressed glass. In order to alleviate the effects of the building height, several projecting oriels are designed as balconies. Bricks have been laid on the prefab roofs, underneath which apartments were built. The ground floors are reserved for shop space, while a free-standing, visually appealing institute for children arose on Voßstraße. Tall trees were prohibited owing to the border installations, while some stairwells acquired frosted glass panes. The residential estate was only completed after the fall of the Wall. The street An der Kolonnade affords the best overview of façade design in the area. The historic Spittelkolonnaden (Spittel Colonnades) were intended to have been assembled here, although today these are located on Dönhoffplatz (Dönhoff Square). Although the buildings have been preserved in their original state and the area is set to achieve conservation status, a demolition permit has been issued for Wilhelmstraße 55–59 (December 2015).

D

North Korean Embassy

Glinkastraße 5–7
Manfred Jäkel, Gerhard Schubring
and collective
1974

This site has no longer been used in its original size since the turning point in early politics in the early 1990s. Since 2011, the former chancellery building has been rented to a hostel. The Büro zum Schutz der Interessen der Demokratischen Volksrepublik Korea (Office for the Protection of the Interests of the Democratic People's Republic of Korea) still operates in the building of the commercial agency, Glinkastraße 5. The complex consists of three parts. The chancellery (the current hostel) obtained strikingly faceted concrete panels with barely visible window frames. Concrete slabs featuring polished natural stone accentuate the verticality of the projecting stairwells at the gable ends, while profiled glass bands provide illumination. The entrance is surmounted by a concrete roof reminiscent of an inverted pagoda. A low-rise building with a conference room

Floor plan of the former chancellery building

Former residential block for the staff of the embassy which is now also used as the chancellery

Former chancellery which is now rented profitably to a hostel

adjoins the embassy at the back. In the rectangular structure along Zietenplatz (Zieten Square), commercial agency offices are on the ground floor, and above are apartments for the staff of the embassy. Its loggias are recessed into the southern façade. Long banks of windows facing the square are only punctuated by concrete columns and three staircase towers.

Together with glazed concrete building blocks, these form an extending wave-band. The eastern part of the building follows the bend in the road. The alleged tunnel between the buildings was neither repudiated nor confirmed. What's remarkable is that the grey of the façade is precisely in keeping with the dreariness of Pyongyang.

D

Photos: Philipp Meuser

Buildings with Arcades

D 077

Charlottenstraße 50–52
Manfred Prasser, Dieter Bankert,
Ernst Wallis, Wolfgang Sebastian
1983

All buildings on the west side were erected as a frame structure and are clad in pre-fab panels. The current hotel served as a guest home for the Akademie der Wissenschaften der DDR (Academy of Sciences of the GDR). Adorned with elaborate mosaics and boasting an elegant shade of white, it is the only building on the square to be in the art nouveau style.

Buildings with Arcades ⌃   D 078
Charlottenstraße 53/54
Manfred Prasser, Günter Boy
1985

It is worth noting the double columns that appear to support the building. The red façade richly adorned with classical stuccoed projections, the steep tiled roof and the striking mansard windows give little indication that these are prefab components. Today's office and commercial building previously served as the residence of the East German faction-party the CDU.

D

Konzerthaus Administration ⌄   D 079
Charlottenstraße 55/56
Manfred Prasser, Peter Kobe et al.
1980–1988

This is arguably the most remarkable new building on the street: perfection in an illusion is achieved since the façade flows with a seamless transition into Schinkel's concert hall and dark grey concrete and golden mosaic tesserae give the two-part building a noble look. The edifice served mainly as the office of the Konzerthaus (Concert Hall) and is still used by Berlin-based musical institutions today.

Source: Leibniz-Institut (IRS)

Photo: Martin Püschel

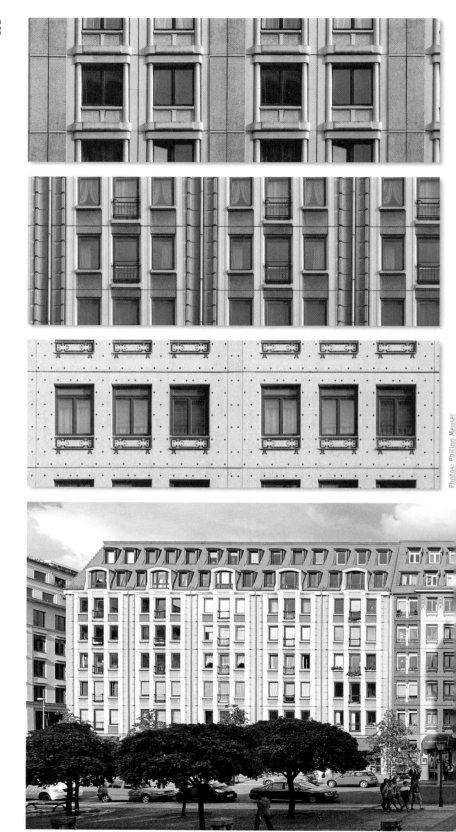

Photos: Philipp Meuser

East Side of Gendarmenmarkt D 080

Markgrafenstraße 39–41
Manfred Prasser, Matthias Borner
1988

This block consists of four architecturally significant residential buildings extending to Französische and Jägerstraße. Shops and restaurants which were conceived from the outset are situated on the ground floor, although some are on the first floor. The remaining storeys accommodate 120 apartments according to the principle of WBS 70. These are in part very spacious – especially those in the lofts – and are today municipal property. Despite substantial criticism having been made of the fact they are not socialist enough, the architects insisted upon different façades so that these bow in their fragmentation to the outstanding ensemble in the middle of the square. Worthy of note is the mosaic façade of the central part of the building which seems almost extravagant in its attention to detail. Another affront was also accorded: the residential building situated on the corner of Markgrafenstraße and Jägerstraße has an implied corner tower – as was the custom in Imperial Berlin (and as established by building law).

Photo: Martin Püschel

D

Photo: Philipp Meuser

Industrially prefabricated concrete columns on the façade of the Hilton hotel

D

Dom-Hotel

Mohrenstraße 30
Bernd Seidel
1990

The building complex with the frame construction was built between 1989 and 1990 for the State-run Interhotel in the GDR and was finally opened at the end of 1990 as the Dom-Hotel. In 1991, the American Hilton chain purchased the building with about 600 rooms,

conference and meeting rooms, a club, spa areas and seven restaurants. Originally there was an eight-storey atrium. The façade projects a strong vertical effect and is designed along the lines of classicism. The first floor is conceived as a spacious *bel étage* borne by columns with rows of rising windows and an opulent mansard roof. A likewise industrially prefabricated car park with administrative facilities on the attic level adjoins the hotel at the back.

AfEP Headquarters «

Mohrenstraße / Jerusalemer Straße
Unknown
ca. 1989

Although the frame construction with façades made of concrete panels was originally conceived for the Amt für Erfindungs- und Patentwesen der DDR (Office for Inventions and Patents of the GDR, AfEP), it was never completed amidst the turmoil of the Wall coming down and the ensuing political upheaval. The façade with its angled concrete relief panels and three oriels made of cupric oxide glass has been preserved almost in its original state. Since its conversion by Eller + Eller Architekten (1997–2001), it has become part of the office of the Bundesjustizministerium (Federal Ministry of Justice).

Spitteleck
Seydelstraße / Wallstraße
Eckart Schmidt
1985

D 083

D

Constituting an almost brutalist bastion on Spittelmarkt, the historic southern side of the market square is bordered by the severe arc of the building. Its terraces facing the old buildings create a tiered arrangement. Despite its giant dimensions, the small-scale development addresses its surroundings through projecting and recessed balconies in relief concrete. In the year 1987, Eckart Schmidt was awarded the *Architekturpreis Berlin* (Berlin Architecture Prize) for the building with 295 (324 after its refurbishment)

apartments featuring indoor kitchens. The architect occupied a two-storey studio apartment on Wallstraße. In 2015, the complex was renovated by the communal housing association Wohnungsbaugesellschaft Mitte (WBM) in collaboration with the architect. The façades and colours are based on the originals and the concrete balconies were restored – even the courtyard side was clad in plaster with pebbles and panel wall joints. A kindergarten was originally located on the ground floor, while the stairwells culminate in storey-high concrete panels with children's motifs and those depicting natural themes. These were removed due to new emergency exits, although two of them were restored in the courtyard.

Source: Wohnungsbaugesellschaft Mitte Archives

Photo: Martin Püschel

Idyllic suburban scene three minutes by car from the Berlin Stadtschloss/Humboldt-Forum

Standard Design Q3
*Annenstraße/Dresdener Straße
Arno Lokczynski (architecture),
Werner Dutschke (urban design)
1959*

This building type featuring transverse walls in block construction was chosen as the provisional type for the centre of Berlin in the late 1950s. Q3 stands for transverse-wall-type No. 3. Prior to 1969, 28,600 apartments were built in variant A (Q3A). The lifting equipment of post-war years could only bear 0.8 tonnes maximum with the result that a wall would consist of multiple blocks. Owing to a lack of materials, brick chippings from bombed-out buildings were added to the concrete. A reinforced concrete ring beam extends around the window openings. The inner transverse walls are separated by a distance of 2.40 m or 3.60 m. Apartments acquired indoor bathrooms, outdoor kitchens and furnace heating. French windows or balconies were also used. Many of the gable walls were subsequently fitted with a thermal insulation system. Last but not least, the exterior walls were plastered upon assembly in order to conceal the panel wall joints. A slightly pitched roof lent the prefab buildings a more traditional appearance. The landscaping within the territory of Dresener Straße particularly illustrates the garden-city character intended for the centre of Berlin.

Source: Leibniz-Institut (IRS)

Photo: Philipp Meuser

D

Source: Landesarchiv Berlin

Fischerinsel

D 085

Fischerinsel
Joachim Näther, Peter Schweizer,
Manfred Zache (urban design),
Hans-Peter Schmiedel,
Manfred Zumpe et al. (high-rises)
1970

Source: Waltraud Volk: Berlin – Hauptstadt der DDR. Berlin 1980

Welcome to the oldest part of Berlin – the old city of Cölln on the Spree! It wasn't until the late 1960s (more than twenty years after the Second World War) that the remains of the old buildings were cleared and individual façades displaced by significant edifices on today's Wallstraße. A hotel and five non-standard designs for the prefab building type WHH-GT were originally planned following the sweep of the Spree Canal under the provisional title of Fischerkiez (Fisher Village). The acronym WHH-GT means residential high-rise large-panel construction. Those types on Fischerinsel (Fisher Island) each have 240 apartments over twenty-one storeys. A sixth dual high-rise from WHH-GT ended up being built in lieu of the hotel. Beside a day-care centre and a swimming pool, there is also the canteen of the GDR Bauministerium (Ministry of Construction) named the Großgaststätte Ahornblatt (Great Maple Leaf Restaurant), as shown on the stamp. In spite of its listed status, the building

by the master of concrete shell structures, Ulrich Müther, was demolished in 2000 and replaced by featureless new buildings (Getraudenstraße). Fischerinsel continues to be targeted by urban planners and a higher urban density is set to be established, primarily along Mühlendamm.

Photos: Philipp Meuser

D

View of high-rises on Fischerinsel and the Ahornblatt, 1999

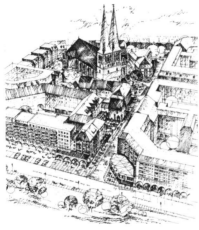

Nikolaiviertel D 086

Poststraße/Probststraße
Ehrhardt Gißke (coordinator),
Günter Stahn, Wolfgang Woigk,
Reiner Rauer
1987

To mark the 750th anniversary of Berlin, the GDR government decided to rebuild Nikolaikirche (St. Nicholas' Church) and its surroundings by historic standards. Distinctive elements are the prefab buildings with their arcades and gables in a canal style that never previously existed. The arcades comprising concrete transverse slabs acquired gothic ribbed vaults with candelabra, while the display windows were designed as tiny oriels. The ornamentation was made of artificial stone. The approximately 800 prefab apartments were built from supporting transverse slabs, on site in a monolithic design, or according to the principle of WBS 70. Textured exposed aggregate concrete and projecting concrete slabs lend a bold structure to the discernible prefab façades. Even the pseudo-old structures on Nikolaikirchplatz (St. Nicholas' Church Square) and Mühlendamm are prefab buildings with reconstructed – contrived – medieval façades. A few buildings were rebuilt in almost original condition, such as Ephraimpalais (Ephraim Palace), whose façade survived the war by being placed in storage. Replicas also include the tavern Nußbaum (Nut Tree) and the Gerichtslaube (Court Pergola). Less elaborate façades can primarily be seen facing Marx-Engels-Forum, while the frieze of the Rotes Rathaus (Red Town Hall) is continued from a socialist perspective in a frieze by Gerhard Thieme. Worthy-of-note are the so-called swallows' nests on Rathausstraße and Poststraße. The projections on the first floor serve as seating bays in a restaurant and were reconstructed true to the original design in 2015.

D

Source: Bundesarchiv (photo 183-U0622)

New Building Complex on Rathausstraße

D 087

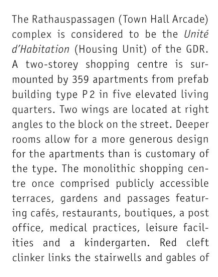

Rathausstraße
Heinz Graffunder with
Dietmar Kunztsch, Lothar Köhler,
Walter Wenzel (architecture),
Joachim Näther, Peter Schweizer
and collective (urban design)
1972

The Rathauspassagen (Town Hall Arcade) complex is considered to be the *Unité d'Habitation* (Housing Unit) of the GDR. A two-storey shopping centre is surmounted by 359 apartments from prefab building type P 2 in five elevated living quarters. Two wings are located at right angles to the block on the street. Deeper rooms allow for a more generous design for the apartments than is customary of the type. The monolithic shopping centre once comprised publicly accessible terraces, gardens and passages featuring cafés, restaurants, boutiques, a post office, medical practices, leisure facilities and a kindergarten. Red cleft clinker links the stairwells and gables of the living quarters with the Rotes Rathaus (Red Town Hall), while the facetted façade is based on pre-war buildings found on Alexanderplatz (Alexander Square). The particularly light-coloured concrete façade was achieved by means of white marble chips and additionally adorned with blue Reichenbach glass mosaics. Windows extending almost from the floor to the ceiling visually incorporate the living rooms into the sprawling open spaces around the Fernsehturm (TV Tower) from the inside. In common with the town hall tower, the living quarters are also set back from the lower building front. The inherent character of the shopping centre has been completely lost since its conversion as of 2002; only the roof gardens were partially rebuilt. Terraces and gardens can still be witnessed above today's medical practices, while the central route across the passages follows the historic path of Klosterstraße. In spite of thermal insulation, the living quarters have been returned to their original design – the fact that concrete panels are no longer used is only visible up close.

D

166

South End of Memhardstraße D 088
Memhardstraße 1–5
Klaus Bläsing and collective
1984

The building with 148 apartments is a non-standard design according to the principle of WBS 70. By means of clinker brick slips, its original façade was based proportionally on the listed Grenander-haus (Grenander House) with which it forms a housing block. The monolithic ground floor accommodates shop space, while offices originally occupied the first floor. The delivery zone for the Centrum department store (today known as Galeria Kaufhof) is accessed from Rosa-Luxemburg-Straße, through the building and underneath the main street. The roof of this area forms the basis for the immense garden on the second floor of the residential building – the apartments facing the courtyard on the second floor thus seem to be located on the ground floor. The complex was renovated in 2015 and lost its proportions owing to the omission of most of the panel wall joints. Today, the oriels cantilever from the plaster façade in a somewhat low-brow fashion. The roof garden is to be rebuilt, while the inscription of the Memhardt Plan – the oldest city map of Berlin-Cölln – has been appropriated for the gable towards Karl-Liebknecht-Straße.

North End of Memhardstraße D 089
Memhardstraße 2, 6 and 8
Klaus Bläsing and collective
1983

The colossus spanning up to thirteen storeys is a frame construction. Almost all of the 126 apartments are maisonettes – only in house No. 2 are there spacious apartments in mezzanines on one floor. House No. 6 was added last – today, the entrance is thus situated in the Haus des Berliner Verlages (Berlin Publishing House) on Karl-Liebknecht-Straße. Furthermore, this section of building forms a constructional unit with Pressecafé, today a steakhouse. The restaurant itself occupies an elevated cube which seems to float above the street, while the kitchen and building technology have been integrated into the first floor of the residential building. The stair towers never received a façade and remain unfurnished. There are many myths surrounding the window in the gable of house No. 8, but it is merely a result of circumstances. This part consists – almost – entirely of one-bedroom apartments, with the exception of the two upper storeys. Maisonette apartments are once again situated there, although there is a room in lieu of an escape exit. The concrete panels of the façade were fortified with crushed quartz, allowing the building to glint in the sun. Today, the building has a brownish appearance owing to the accumulation of dirt. The complex acquired a mere seven-storey annex on Rosa-Luxemburg-Straße in order to establish a visual connection to the intricate historic building there. All urban development plans propose the demolition of the fully-let building, although at the present time this is not politically feasible.

Photo: Philipp Meuser

Photo: Hans-Erich Bogatzky

Standard Design QP

Karl-Marx-Allee
Josef Kaiser and collective;
Edmund Collein, Werner Dutschke
(urban design)
1965

D 090

The standard design QP was exclusively built in Berlin. The acronym stands for *Querplatte* (transverse panel), a design with only 3.60 m wide rooms, thus prohibiting architects from placing shops on the ground floor. The series QP59 initially had five storeys, whereas the more common series QP61 and 64 had eight featuring lifts to the penultimate floor. This was followed later by ten storeys for QP64, such as on Karl-Marx-Allee. The series was extended by

QP71 and following, with radically different floor plans. Stairwells and waste disposal rooms are located on the rear side and naturally illuminated. The narrow windowed kitchen and the small interior bathroom share an axis until housing series QP64. Façade panels with colourful ceramics, cornice borders and claddings on balconies were originally used. No one house is the same as another. Projecting balconies alternate with large French windows to lend structure to the façades. The main entrance doors, house numbers, balustrades and even the screws were custom-designed. Balconies almost covering the entire gable are a special design feature for series QP64. A façade which has almost been preserved in its original style is visible on Schillingstraße 27–29.

Source: Landesarchiv Berlin

Photo: Martin Püschel

D

Leninplatz

Platz der Vereinten Nationen
Hermann Henselmann,
Wilfried Stallknecht
1970

In the shape of the winding prefab buildings named *Schlange* (Snake) and *Bumerang* (Boomerang), the architects brought "the round into the square". The curves had to have the same inclination since the house-building factory did not want to change the crane track. A QP-slab in green with a department store fitted in front – the most modern one in the GDR – makes up the southern frontier. The backdrop for Nikolai W. Tomski's towering Lenin monument is comprised by the leafy mound of rubble in Friedrichshain and a high-rise of the WHH-GT type (project engineer: Heinz Mehlan). It has three tiers over twenty-five storeys and follows the rising flag of the monument. The ensemble featuring 1,250 apartments is a listed building – unfortunately Lenin has been absent since 1992 to make it ideologically correct.

D

Monument of Lenin by Nikolai V. Tomsky (1970)

Source: Bundesarchiv (photo 183-1984-0212-004)

Ernst-Thälmann-Park

D 092

*Danziger/Greifswalder Straße
Ehrhardt Gißke, Eugen Schröter
(urban design), Helmut Stingl,
Dietrich Kabisch, Marianne Battke,
Dorothea Krause et al. (architecture)
1986*

To mark Ernst Thälmann's 100th birthday and Berlin's 750th anniversary, the gas works on Dimitroffstraße were transformed into a green oasis covering 25 ha. Apartments, service facilities and cultural institutions were also built around the Thälmann monument. The high-rise WHH-GT84/85 was thus designed with a grid of 3,600 mm. Towers with twelve, fifteen and eighteen storeys were created on the left and right of the monument. Building services are located on the monolithic ground floor. There are eight one- to four-room apartments on each fully assembled upper storey. Compared to other residential high-rises, the assortment of elements was reduced by more than half, with built-in heat recovery systems a standard feature. WBS 70/11 was reduced to eight storeys owing to the surrounding old buildings. Three angled groups featuring glazed loggias, corner terraces and four studio apartments were created. The balconies were executed in so-called demolition concrete (corrugated). Everything was planned down to the last detail, including interior and exterior colour schemes alike, as well as custom-designed house numbers. Inspired by the renovated historic administrative buildings, the prefab buildings were adorned with décor comprising clinker brick slips, stone entrances and pergolas. The outcome also includes a well thought-out system of pathways, a swimming pool, restaurants, a cultural centre, kindergartens, a planetarium, an adventure playground worth seeing and a pond featuring a waterfall. The ensemble has been listed under a conservation order since 2014.

Source: Bundesarchiv (photo 183-1989-0416_003)

Photo: Martin Püschel

Thälmann monument by Lev Kerbel

D

Photo: Philipp Meuser

Series P 2 (Prototype)

Erich-Kuttner-Straße 9–15
Wilfried Stallknecht, Achim Felz,
Herbert Kuschy .
1963

D 093

This building type sets completely new benchmarks and was named the winner in the competition to design housing from 1963. Inside are stairwells, bathrooms and kitchens. Wide window fronts are reserved for living spaces, while loggias offer a second living room in summer. Windows almost extending from the floor to the ceiling were also applied in subsequent designs. The revolutionary aspect lay in the kitchen which was connected to the living room via a custom-designed cabinet by Wilfried Stallknecht: cooking, dining and living form a single unity, while domestic tasks are carried out in the midst of family life. The original building with gas burners was designed with its own closed chimney system, the SE-duct, and a gravity exhaust ventilation system without ventilators. Bathrooms were elevated to the shell building as fully prefab sanitary blocks. Further developments in P 2 come with up to twelve storeys. The first experimental building featuring an illuminated corridor system and utility rooms was built on Schneeglöckchen-straße. The lifts stop every three storeys and make accessible six apartments each via the stairwell. Floor-to-ceiling built-in cupboards were able to replace the walls between the corridors and bedrooms based on a grid of 6 m.

D

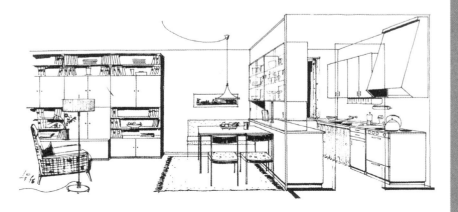

Source: Leibniz-Institut für Regionalentwicklung und Strukturplanung (IRS)

Standard Design WBS 70/5 D 094

Möllendorf-/Rutnikstraße
Erwin Kussat and collective
1973

WBS 70 is the best-known prefab build-ing of the GDR era. No other series under-went so many variants and was built as often. The first ensemble to be realised in Berlin is located on the corner of Möllendorfstraße and Rutnikstraße. The prototype is located in Neubrandenburg. This model for success was created on the basis of studies from 1969 conducted by Wilfried Stallknecht and Achim Felz. The aim was to enable a more rational mass production of component parts. The num-ber after 70 is a reference to the number of storeys. A lift was not necessary until the fifth storey. Five- and six-storey apart-ments were built for the greater part as well as buildings with up to eleven storeys as of 1977. The floor span length is 6 m; all components are based on a vertical

and horizontal grid of 1.20 m. Walls made of ordinary concrete and ceilings made of prestressed concrete with a load level of 6.3 tonnes were used. Fully assembled, the prefab bathroom cubicles were elevated to the shell building. The maintenance shaft with pipes and vents was shared with the kitchen. Almost all designs for WBS 70 have kitchens positioned along one of the exterior walls; however, the model on Rutnikstraße has an inner kitchen with a hatch which is indicated by the miss-ing window next to the living room. The grid of the panel is still clearly visible on the façade. Bedrooms and nurseries face the street, while living rooms with bal-conies (subsequently added, originally about 1.20 m deep) can be seen to the south overlooking the garden.

Source: Leibniz-Institut (IRS)

Series L4 (Prototype)

Marksburgstraße/Ilsestraße
Leopold Wiel
1956/57

D 095

D

The series encompasses buildings similar to those from the Q3 series, albeit in longitudinal construction. The 30 cm wide exterior wall blocks made of lightweight concrete weigh 0.75 tonnes, while the thickness of the interior walls is 20 cm. Reinforced concrete hollow-core slabs were mainly used for the ceilings. French windows or loggias were also commissioned, depending on the design, but as a rule these were recessed into the façade. The central hot-water supply and heating were easy to operate and the design for the roof was either sloping (75°) or flat (8°). Bathrooms are located internally or externally according to the section, whereas all kitchens and stairwells are on the outside. The façades were

often left unplastered, in contrast to the Q3 series. In the meantime, the L4 prototype has been substantially renovated so that the heat insulation composite system conceals the gaps of the large-block method. In addition, several buildings acquired winter gardens between the gables which led to both a higher level of living comfort and a loss in authenticity.

Splanemann-Siedlung Project D 096
Splanemannstraße
Martin Wagner
1926

The Betondorp (Concrete Village) in Amsterdam, a housing estate based on the Atterbury system, gave Martin Wagner, director of urban development in the city of Berlin, no peace. He saw the solution to the housing shortage as lying in prefabrication; Berlin's first prefab housing estate was thus created under his leadership. The two- to three-storey buildings were built in Friedrichsfelde. Large panels were poured into wooden moulds on site and put into position by a crane. Each of the triple-layer panels measured 3 m x 7.5 m and weighed over 7 tonnes. Only the walls, however, were built using the prefab large-panel construction method, whereas chimneys, ceilings, roofs and basements were of conventional design. Loggias, internal WCs and bathrooms provided an

otherwise unaccustomed level of comfort, heated by tiled stoves. Tenant gardens were laid out behind the buildings. The technology used back then was still in development, the panels were too heavy, the serial size too small and the repetition of the façades met with rejection among the population. Stone was eventually built on stone, as originally planned with the Splanemann estate. At one time, 138 apartments were assembled; today there remain 118. The housing estate was renovated and is a listed building.

Source: Die Wohnungswirtschaft,

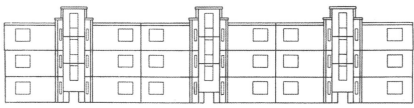

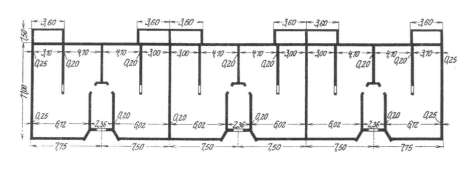

Kinderkombination 90/180

Erieseering 4–6
WBK Erfurt et al.,
Walter Sutkowski (artist)
1975

D 097

D

A *Kinderkombination* was a special institution in the former GDR which hosted a nursery and a kindergarten under one roof. In 1968, the house-building factory Erfurt developed a standard series as a care facility housing ninety crèches, or 180 childcare places. This was then further developed, although it remained essentially the same. A two-storey and a parallel one-storey wing were built in the 2-Mp-method of assembly, connected by two glazed corridors. Administration services were located between the wings housing care services. Entrances were often marked by concrete building blocks or ceramics with animal or playful motifs. This building type was replicated hundredfold in the GDR.

Photos: Philipp Meuser

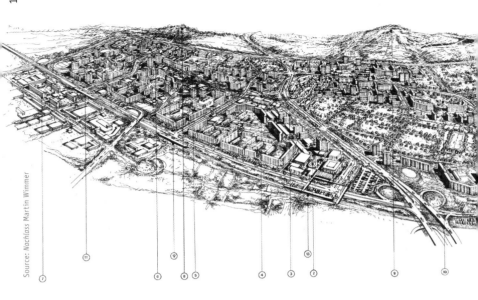

Source: *Nachlass Martin Wimmer*

Photo: Philipp Meuser

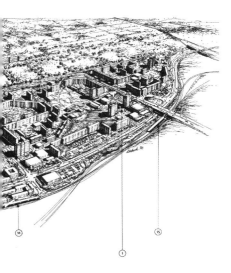

Marzahn Housing Complex D 099

Allee der Kosmonauten,
Marzahner Promenade
Heinz Graffunder, Helmut Stiegl,
Peter Schweizer, Wolf R. Eisentraut et al.
1976–1990

Marzahn arose as the ninth urban district to alleviate the housing shortage in East Berlin. The first housing estate in the south, at Springpfuhl, was completed in 1978. The population of Marzahn increased to 172,00 prior to 1990. Long rectangular buildings from the angled WBS 70 are prevalent in the district with lots of greenery. Alongside these arose very few types, such as WBS Q P 71-R, a successor to the Q P series. High-rises may be found at prominent points, such as at railway stations and shopping venues – for example, there are residential towers in frame construction at Springpfuhl, prefab towers from WHH-GT 84/86 in a fan-like form on the shopping boulevard of Marzahner Promenade and examples of WHH-GT 18/21 at the historic centre of the village. It is worth noting the meadow-like centre of the village preserved in its original style with the mill and church (the street Alt-Marzahn) amidst the prefab buildings. New shopping centres were built after the fall of the Wall and a large-scale refurbishment was carried out. The Ahrensfelder Terrassen (Ahrensfeld Terraces) are regarded as a model project for the decommissioning plans dating back to around 2000. Individual storeys of prefab buildings were demolished, floor plans changed and 1,689 apartments were turned into 409 rented flats and thirty-eight owner-occupied apartments (Havemannstraße 7–22). Following desertions after the fall of the Wall, the number of inhabitants is now increasing again and new buildings are emerging between the residential blocks. The vacancy rate was only 1.6 per cent in 2014 – thus on the same level as the hipster Kreuzberg district. Today, Marzahn has made it into West German awareness as a synonym for monotonous prefab buildings from the late phase of the GDR. Nonetheless, the district is a global pioneer for the successful refurbishment of a socialist model estate.

Former Rathaus Marzahn D 098

Helene-Weigel-Platz
Wolf R. Eisentraut, Karin Bock,
Bernd Walther
1988

The new arrangement of available standard prefab elements enabled an architectural collective from the construction and assembly combine IHB (Ingenieur-hochbau Berlin) to create this unique building, a former town hall. Longitudinal ceramic panels and potted plants lend a pronounced structure to the façade. Bright offices were created inside – therefore, the visitor did not have to force their way across confined corridors. The light-flooded atrium with a circumferential stair as well as works of art are not to be missed. One slightly bewildering feature is a striking ceramic panel which can be found in the courtyard of the building. A concrete worker arduously arranged light and dark tiles in a chequered pattern (undesired by the architect). The art featured around the building was created by the sculptor Peter Makolies. The entrance portal, which is unfortunately lost, can be traced back to a design by the metalwork designers Jan Skuin and Rüdiger Roehl. The edifice has been a listed building since 2008.

D

Museumswohnung
Hellersdorfer Straße 179
1987

D 100

The Museumswohnung (Museum Flat) owned by a municipally owned housing company promises pure nostalgia for the former East Germany. The three-room apartment covering 61 m² had a full rental fee of 109 GDR marks. Completed in 1986, it serves today as a relic of a true prefab building in Hellersdorf. Those who have never set foot in a prefab apartment can experience the economical floor plan and examine original bathroomware and fitted kitchens from the 1980s. In several places, no wallpaper has been put up and the texture of load-bearing and non-load-bearing concrete panels from a WBS 70 comes to the fore. Savings were made as of the 1970s – again, the concrete has not attained the quality of previous years, especially regarding noise insulation. The apartment was furnished with everything with which the fund of

the socialist past had to offer – from the Foron fridge and Dedoron apron to the velour couch. It remains questionable whether GDR citizens really were provided with such furnishings, although it is always worth seeing to make you smile and may surprise you (or the one or the other childhood memory).

D

Photos: Philipp Meuser

Index of Architects

Sorted according to project number

Index of Buildings

Sorted according to project number

Index of Streets

Sorted according to project number

Authors

Dominik Schendel
Born 1986, studied architecture in
Hamburg, Vienna and Berlin. Worked
at Hermann Czech in Vienna as well as
at Volker Staab and Sackmann Payer
Architects in Berlin. His extensive know-
how of the urban and architectural history of his adopted city is incorporated
into the *Architectural Guide Berlin*, which
is written with great passion.

Philipp Meuser
Born 1969, Architect BDA and Publisher.
Has conducted research on prefab mass
housing and Socialist Modernism, among
other things.

Martin Püschel
Born 1981, Editor of the *Plattenbau*-
cultural portal *jeder-qm-du.de* of the
Wohnungsbaugesellschaft Mitte (WBM).

The *Deutsche Nationalbibliothek* list this
publication in the *Deutschen National-
bibliografie;* detailed bibliographic data
are available on the Internet at
http://dnb.d-nb.de.

ISBN 978-3-86922-547-0

© 2016 by DOM publishers, Berlin
www.dom-publishers.com

Translation
Clarice Knowles

Graphic Design
Dominik Schendel

Maps
Senatsverwaltung für Stadtentwicklung
und Umweltschutz, Landeskartenwerk

Printing
Tiger Printing (Hong Kong) Co., Ltd.
www.tigerprinting.hk

Picture Credits
Unless otherwise indicated, photos,
plans, visualisations and other
graphics were supplied from the author
and co-authors or the respective
architectural practices.

*A general approach to denoting street
names has been adopted, whereby words
such as Straße and Allee have not been
translated owing to common usage.*

Catalogue
Winter 2016/2017

Books made by Architects

DOM
publishers

Starchitects @ DOM publishers

Conversations with Peter Eisenman
The Evolution of Architectural Style

Vladimir Belogolovsky
210 × 230 mm
152 pages, 130 images
Softcover
ISBN 978-3-86922-531-9
€ 28.00

ISBN 978-3-86922-531-9

9 783869 225319

Peter Eisenman's architecture carries many layers and meanings; one question leads to the next and one conversation provokes another. Vladimir Belogolovsky's new book highlights three separate conversations he had with the architect at his New York City studio. These conversations are part of the author's ongoing interview project he initiated in 2002, discussing architecture with over 100 leading international architects. "Peter Eisenman is in the bloodline of Palladio, Le Corbusier, and Robert Venturi, and in this book of brutally honest conversations between him and critic Vladimir Belogolovsky pithy assertions emerge, sometimes in contradiction, as Belogolovosky sympathetically questions this authority, one whose deep commitment to his art, over fifty years, has helped change contemporary architecture. (…) Eisenman bemoans the fact that celebrity architects have supplanted such authorities, that is, authors of a critical architecture that reflects on its own language. All art languages must do this, an important insight of semiotics in the 1960s when Eisenman first started critical practice." (Charles Jencks)

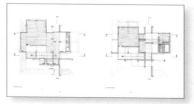

Architecture in Archives
The Collection of the Academy of Arts

NEW

Academy of Arts Berlin (ed.)
235 × 275 mm, 560 pages
900 images, hardcover
ISBN 978-3-86922-552-4
€ 68.00

ISBN 978-3-86922-552-4

9 783869 225524

The Akademie der Künste (Academy of Arts) in Berlin has carried out its task of promoting the arts in Germany since the year it was founded in 1696. From the outset, master builders have been eligible to become members. The architect Hans Scharoun laid the groundwork for establishing the architectural archive. As the first post-war president of the academy in West Berlin, he was eager to document twentieth-century architecture in the Archive. Besides the story lying behind the assembly of a collection, this publication presents all seventy-one archives and eighty collections, including short biographies of the originators and the nature and scope of inventories. The Preußische Akademie (Prussian Academy) is represented among other things by drawings by Friedrich Gilly from the end of the eighteenth century. Expressionist designs by Bruno Taut, Alfons Anker, Paul Goesch and Adolf Behne in particular are to be found in rich abundance. In common

with the archives of Richard Ermisch, Paul Baumgarten and Thilo Schoder, these offer a chronicle of the 1920s. One focus of the collection is devoted to the archives of Second World War émigré architects, among them Adolf Rading, Gabriel Epstein, Julius Posener and Konrad Wachsmann. The post-war period and the booming 1960s are represented by the archives of Hermann Henselmann, Walter Rossow, Bernhard Hermkes, Werner Hebebrand, Werner Düttmann and Heinz Graffunder. Archives and collections which can be traced back beyond the turn of the twenty-first century emerged from Jörg Schlaich, Kurt Ackermann, Szyszkowitz + Kowalski and Valentien + Valentien. On offer for the first time is an overview in print form of these archives acquired by the Academy up to the present day – archives of architects, engineers, landscape architects and architectural photographers and critics alike. This publication presents an excerpt from around half a million documents.

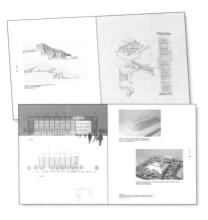

Container and Modular Buildings
Construction and Design Manual

Cornelia Dörries/Sarah Zahradnik
225 × 280 mm, 240 pages
300 images
Softcover
ISBN 978-3-86922-515-9
€ 38.00

ISBN 978-3-86922-515-9
9 783869 225159

Bold and unconventional ideas are called for if the intention is to steer the debate on temporary accommodation for refugees in a new direction offering high-quality solutions. From eccentric experiments all the way to projects which have already been realized, international design teams present their work between the twin poles of unconventional developments and life-saving shelters in this compilation of case studies, *Container and Modular Buildings*.

Not all of these are applicable to the current refugee crisis, since that which digital nomads find hip constitutes harsh reality for others. Yet alongside playful follies, we can find miniature architectural structures for the homeless as well as outpatient medical stations which offer a response to social problems and space shortages. The photographic material puts forward ideas as to how more can be done than the mere assembling of containers.

Project *Eco-Pod*, architects: Eric Höweler, J. Meejin Yoon

Hidden Urbanism
Architecture and Design of the Moscow Metro 1935–2015

**Sergey Kuznetsov/Alexander Zmeul/
Erken Kagarov**
*Edited by Philipp Meuser and
Anna Martovitskaya*
235 × 305 mm, 352 pages, 500 images
Hardcover, ISBN 978-3-86922-412-1
€ 98.00

NEW

ISBN 978-3-86922-412-1
9 783869 224121

The Moscow metro comprises a route network with a total length of 320 km and is the most fascinating underground transportation system in the world. Each year more than 2.4 billion passengers use almost 200 stations which are rich in architectural design. The aim is for a further 80 km – that is a quarter of the current network – to be connected by 2017. The metro of the Russian capital is thus on the threshold of an enlargement which will be the largest in its history.

This elaborately designed illustrated book focuses on the architecture and its associated design from the signage, to the logo branding, to the many printed materials. Three text contributions consider the underground world of traffic engineering in terms of construction history, from the point of view of the Chief Architect of Moscow, architectural history and the design bureau which lent the metro its unmistakable character.

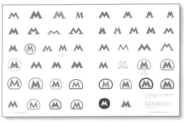

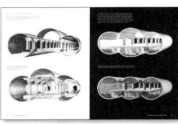

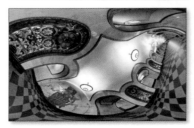

Towards a Typology of Soviet Mass Housing

Prefabrication in the USSR 1955–1991

NEW

Philipp Meuser/Dimitrij Zadorin
165 × 235 mm, 456 pages, 1,000 images
Hardcover, card game, model
(The Limited Collector's Edition)
ISBN 978-3-86922-458-9
€ 68.00

ISBN 978-3-86922-458-9

9 783869 224589

Soviet mass housing is a contradictory but unique phenomenon. It is usually blamed for creating the most monotonous built environment in the history of mankind, thus constituting a symbol of individual suppression and dejection. The construction programme launched in the post-Stalinist era was the largest undertaken in modern architectural history worldwide. At the same time, Soviet mass housing fulfilled a colossal social role, providing tens of millions of families with their own apartments. It shaped the culture and everyday life of nearly all Soviet citizens. Yet, due to the very scale of construction, it managed to evolve into a complex world denoting an abundance of myths and secrets, achievements and failures. Soviet mass housing is indisputably intriguing, but nevertheless it is still neglected as a theme of research. The authors aim to identify the most significant mass housing series in this Limited Collector's Edition.

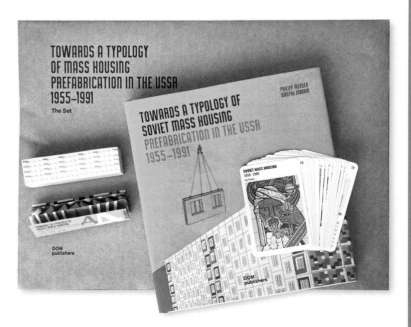

Construction and Design Manuals

Practice-related information, exemplary buildings and inspiration in an attractive design and a handy format: with its didactic, user-oriented concept, the *Construction and Design Manual* series offers everything architects need for construction project solutions.

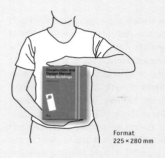

Format
225 × 280 mm

Sample pages from: Construction and Design Manual: School Buildings

Theory
Explanatory texts provide background information and impart historical, typological and planning principles.

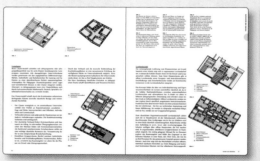

Sample pages from: Construction and Design Manual: Theatres and Concert Halls

Practice
Selected examples of international projects demonstrate the practical implementation of theoretical principles.

Reference Works for Instructors and Learners

Sample pages from: Construction and Design Manual: Architectural Renderings

Practice
Selected examples of international projects demonstrate the practical implementation of theoretical principles.

Sample pages from: Construction and Design Manual: Building Engineering

Details
Individual details in relation to construction materials or assembly parts impart constructional principles.

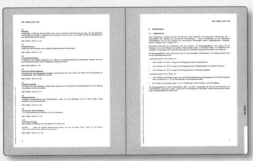

Sample pages from: Construction and Design Manual: Accessible Architecture

Standards and guidelines
Where appropriate, design manuals are compiled as a commentary. Accordingly, we endeavour to include international standards such as the original text of the relevant DIN, Eurocode, ANSI, BS or ISO.

Sample pages from: Construction and Design Manual: Townhouses

Costs and typologies
A comparison of construction costs for certain typologies provides information on the cost estimation of planned buildings.

Prefabricated Housing
Construction and Design Manual

Philipp Meuser
225 × 280 mm, 456 pages
900 images
Hardcover
ISBN 978-3-86922-427-5
€ 78.00

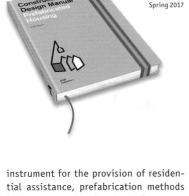

NEW

Spring 2017

ISBN 978-3-86922-427-5

9 783869 224275

Prefabricated housing has long since ceased to mean the disfigurement of the urban landscape with monotonous grey boxes. Particularly in Central Europe and Russia, modern assembly methods and 100 years of experience in planning prefabricated buildings and constructing with large panels are experiencing a renaissance. Whereas predominantly in Moscow – the largest European metropolis with seventeen million – prefabricated housing is an essential instrument for the provision of residential assistance, prefabrication methods in Germany and Switzerland, for example, are used to build exclusive properties. This construction manual examines the potential of prefabricated housing on structural, historical and architectural grounds. In addition to an insight into the methods of production and assembly, roughly twenty selected examples provide a contribution to the discussion on affordable housing.

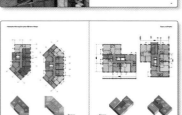

Drawing for Landscape Architects
Construction and Design Manual

Second edition

NEW

Sabrina Wilk
225 × 280 mm, 360 pages
1,200 images, hardcover
ISBN 978-3-86922-535-7
€ 68.00

ISBN 978-3-86922-535-7

Few other professions can match landscape architecture's requirement graphically to represent and communicate so much content and so many ideas. From large-scale master-plans and strategic visions, design concepts and outdoor experiences, to specific vegetation and precise construction details – at some point everything has to be explained on paper. This second edition of the manual focuses on two areas which, even in the age of digital media, are still staples of the profession: orthographic projections and black-line drawings. Intended to be both instructional and inspirational, this book covers the basics of landscape architectural representation, hand drawing and sketching in an easy to understand way, encouraging readers to draw their ideas and develop their own graphic style. Showcased in these pages are many drawings from international landscape architecture offices offering practical guidance and numerous examples in key thematic areas.

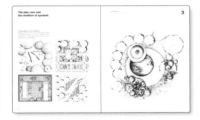
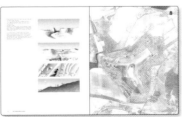

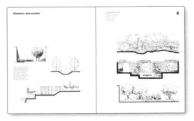

The Life of an Architect ...
... and what he leaves behind

Mike Hermans
245 × 134 mm, 136 pages
Hardcover
ISBN 978-3-86922-440-4
€ 18.00

ISBN 978-3-86922-440-4

9 783869 224404

This title is about the life of architect Archibald and his daily struggle with his office colleagues, employees, clients, contractors, civil servants, consultants, architecture critics, and other people involved in the building industry. Archibald runs an architecture office with his partner and engineer, Gerald. While Archibald is a visionary and a romantic dreamer with a tendency to idealistic and egocentric behavior, Gerald is the rational one who keeps his feet on the ground. An exploited intern named Ralph; a narrow-minded IT-specialist named John, and a weird Asian cardboard model builder named Mr. Shan also work in their office. Archibald is married to Charlotte, a succesful lawyer who quit her job to help Archibald clean up his administrative mess. They have two children: Archie, his six-year-old son who wants to be the best architect in the world and Charly, a smart-mouthed ten-year-old daughter with a strong dislike for everything regarding art.

Basics Series
Architectural History and Theory

Format
210 × 230 mm

The aim of the *Basics* series is to scrutinise critically the debate on architecture and urban development and also to help shape it. The series creates a platform for established authors and committed young researchers who publish texts in their native language, thus imbuing the series with an international flair.

Academic objective
Proofreading research findings, conference papers and essays so that even authors recognize an improvement is of particular importance to us. Of course, we do not dispense with footnotes or a structured bibliography.

Appealing layout
So far we have breathed a little extra life into very dry topics through typography and graphics. Our graphic artists make use of template layouts, but are also careful to give an individual touch to each separate volume.

Precise drawings and plans
Architecture and urban development are primarily communicated by means of drawings and plans. Therefore, we allow space for drawings where a black line can sometimes be more effective than a colourful 3D rendering.

Large-format colour photographs
Academic texts are easier to read when rhythm is introduced into them via large-format photos, another aspect we set great store by. In brief, we would be delighted for you to approach us with a proposed topic.

Soviet Mass Housing
1958–1980
Top Trumps

Dimitrij Zadorin
37 cards, format 65 × 100 mm
ISBN 978-3-86922-443-5
€ 9.95

Behind the Iron Curtain
Confession of a Soviet Architect

Seismic Modernism
**Architecture and Housing
in Soviet Tashkent**

Felix Novikov
252 pages, 360 images
ISBN 978-3-86922-359-9
€ 28.00

Philipp Meuser
256 pages, 300 images
ISBN 978-3-86922-493-0
€ 28.00

Felix Novikov tells the dramatic story of Soviet architecture, portraying the conditions he worked in and how he collaborated with the government and other participants during the creative process. He explains how Soviet design and planning institutes were organised with reference to the Union of the Architects of the USSR and describes the creative ideals of his generation of architects, who are today identified as Soviet Modernists.

Tashkent is a city redolent with contrasts and paradoxes. Home to the most beautiful prefabricated buildings in the world, it features a prominent urban duality predicated upon the oriental Old City and the Russian New City. Never was this contrast brought into sharper focus than during the 1966 earthquake which left the Old City in ruins. There was one respite: a rebuilding effort which triggered an astonishing upsurge of innovation.

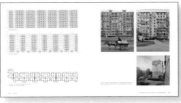

Space Race Archaeologies
Photographs, Biographies, and Design

Pedro Ignacio Alonso (ed.)
128 pages, 130 images
ISBN 978-3-86922-537-1
€ 28.00

As the byproduct of the Cold War, the space race produced a considerable number of objects disseminated in networks, not only in the East and West but also in the global South: rockets, launching pads, satellite tracking stations, astronomical observatories, and several other pieces of design, machineries and infrastructures. These objects are remnants of a modernity tied to secrecy, war deterrence, and mass media associated to outer-space politics.

Design for Space
Soviet and Russian Mission Patches

Alexander Glushko
192 pages, 600 images
ISBN 978-3-86922-328-5
€ 28.00

This book documents a rare collection: almost 250 mission patches worn by Soviet and Russian cosmonauts since 1963. Alexander Glushko, one of the leading specialists in the history of manned space flight and rocket technology in Russia, presents numerous emblems with individual explanations in their applied context: as patches worn on spacesuits. This wide-ranging collection thus brings the history of cosmic heraldry to life.

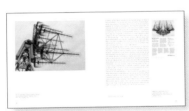

Architectural Guides

Amsterdam ¹
Ankara ¹
Astana ²
Bangkok ²
Berlin ¹²
  Berlin-Mitte ¹
  Berlin Wall ¹
  Berlin Museum Island ¹
Bishkek ¹
Brazil ²
Budapest ¹
Cairo ¹
Chile ²
China ²
Copenhagen ¹
Delhi ²
Dessau
Germany ¹
Düsseldorf ¹
Frankfurt/Main ¹
Gdansk ¹
Hamburg ¹
Havanna ¹
Helsinki ¹²
Hong Kong ¹²
Indonesia ²
Iran ¹
Istanbul ¹
Japan ²
Kazakhstan ¹
Kaunas ¹
Kiev ¹
Leipzig ¹
Lisbon ¹
Milan ²³
Moscow ¹
New York ¹
Nuremberg ¹
Osnabrück ¹
Potsdam ¹
Pyongyang ¹²
Riga ¹²
Rome ¹
Slavutych ²⁴⁵
South Africa ²
St. Petersburg ¹
Taiwan ¹²
Tashkent ¹⁴
Tokyo ¹²
Turin ²
UAE ¹²
Venice ¹²³⁶
Vienna ¹
Vilnius ¹
Warsaw ¹
Wroclaw ²
Yangon ²

1 German
2 English
3 Italian
4 Russian
5 Ukranian
6 French

A city is more than the sum of its buildings.

- ● **New**
- ● Already released
- ○ In preparation

Architectural Guides

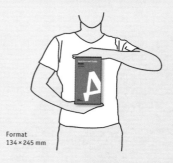

Format
134 × 245 mm

Good architecture can be found across the world. The architectural guides by DOM publishers are far more than just studious architectural reference books – they are expedition guides into the unknown and give way to new perspectives on a sometimes foreign world. Furthermore, they help to understand that the architecture of a city is more than the sum of its attractions.

Text: image ratio
High-resolution photographs and concise texts which not only describe buildings but also comment on them.

Construction documentation
Where appropriate, complex ensembles are also fully documented in the architectural guides.

Drawings
Striking buildings are further explained by floor plans and sections.

Aerial photographs
Photographs from a bird's eye perspective provide a first overview of the city.

Maps
Many architectural guides propose tours which are marked on detailed maps.

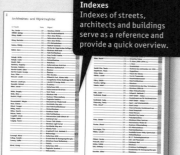

Indexes
Indexes of streets, architects and buildings serve as a reference and provide a quick overview.

Berlin

Architectural Guide

Dominik Schendel
134 × 245 mm, 192 pages
300 images, softcover
ISBN 978-3-86922-547-0
€ 18.00

ISBN 978-3-86922-547-0

Dessau/Wörlitz

Architectural Guide

**Bauhaus Dessau Foundation/
Dessau-Wörlitz Cultural Foundation (ed.)**
134 × 245 mm, 240 pages, 300 images
softcover, ISBN 978-3-86922-371-1
€ 28.00

ISBN 978-3-86922-358-2

In no other place have changing ideologies and urban designs inscribed themselves on the city structure in such a way as in Berlin. This rich collection representing the most diverse urban areas and architectural styles will enable the reader to make a journey through history. Four walks lead to the architectural highlights between Kurfürstendamm in the West and the prefab housing estates in the East. With its extensive maps and full-format aerial photographs, this guide is an ideal companion for discovering the architecture of Berlin.

Dessau may be a mere speck on the map, but the city of Bauhaus still occupies the most important place in the development of the New Building – otherwise known as the *Neues Bauen* – movement. The Garden Kingdom of Dessau Wörlitz (Gartenreich Dessau-Wörlitz) and the Bauhaus School of Design (Bauhaus Hochschule für Gestaltung) have not only bequeathed the city and its surrounds inestimable architectural urban spaces, but also an associated intellectual heritage which has made a lasting impact on the world.

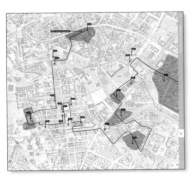

Bangkok
Architectural Guide

December 2016 — NEW

Pattaranan Takkanon
134 × 245 mm, 198 pages
190 images, softcover
ISBN 978-3-86922-358-2
€ 28.00

ISBN 978-3-86922-358-2
9 783869 223582

Chile
Architectural Guide

NEW

Véronique Hours/Fabien Mauduit
134 × 245 mm, 416 pages
800 images, softcover
ISBN 978-3-86922-394-0
€ 38.00

ISBN 978-3-86922-394-0
9 783869 223940

Bangkok is one of the world's most well-known tourist destinations. Travellers are fascinated by its art and cultural diversity and colorful street life. The city's skyline is shaped by a wide range of architectural styles evident in its palaces, temples, historic buildings, all the way to the modern skyscrapers. In spite of the fact that these structures represent the architecture of different eras, they co-exist harmoniously and, at the same time, add spice to a visit to Bangkok.

It is only in these last fifteen years that Chilean architecture has appeared on the international stage, mostly owing to Mathias Klotz, Alejandro Aravena, Smiljan Radic, among others. Le Corbusier also had a great influence on Chilean architects despite never having visited the country. This architectural guide aims to be a non-exhaustive practical directory of the best architecture works of the twentieth and twenty-first centuries in Chile.

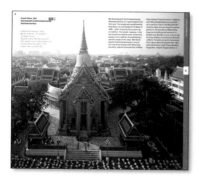

United Arab Emirates

Architectural Guide

Hendrik Bohle/Jan Dimog
134 × 245 mm, 540 pages, 1,000 images
Softcover, ISBN 978-3-86922-508-1
€ 48.00

ISBN 978-3-86922-508-1
9 783869 225081

Covering the record-breaking architecture of Dubai and the majestic gravitas of buildings found in Abu Dhabi, this book unites the diversity and complexity of the United Arab Emirates. The country is increasingly shedding its dependency on oil and gas and investing heavily in trade, logistics, tourism and construction. Masdar City and Yas Island of Abu Dhabi and the artificial islands and towering skyscrapers of Dubai are the most striking results of the economic upswing. In 2020, Dubai will host the Expo – a first in the region.

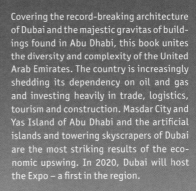

World Atlas of Sustainable Architecture
Building for a Changing Culture and Climate

Ulrich Pfammatter
225 × 280 mm, 584 pages, 2,000 images
Hardcover, ISBN 978-3-86922-282-0
€ 98.00

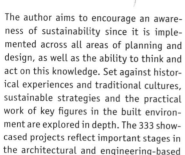

The author aims to encourage an awareness of sustainability since it is implemented across all areas of planning and design, as well as the ability to think and act on this knowledge. Set against historical experiences and traditional cultures, sustainable strategies and the practical work of key figures in the built environment are explored in depth. The 333 showcased projects reflect important stages in the architectural and engineering-based design process.

"A Blessing in Disguise"
War and Town Planning in Europe 1940–1945

Jörn Düwel/Niels Gutschow
240 × 300 mm, 416 pages
800 images, hardcover
ISBN 978-3-86922-295-0
€ 98.00

"There is a sense in which the demolition that is taking place through the war has not yet gone far enough." This astonishing statement was made during World War Two by the American sociologist Lewis Mumford. Although poor hygiene, traffic chaos and social ills had been incessantly pilloried across European countries, only the destruction of war paved the way for a new start. Historians and architects examine post-war urban planning in cities such as Hamburg, Kiev and London.

Urban Catalyst
The Power of Temporary Use

Oswalt/Overmeyer/Misselwitz
165 × 235 mm, 384 pages
200 images, hardcover
ISBN 978-3-86922-261-5
€ 38.00 (second edition)

In many cities, urban wastelands and vacant structures suddenly metamorphose into exuberant places. After the real estate market failed in their initial attempts to develop these, the sites instead became the setting for art galleries, migrant economies, informal markets and nightlife outlets. It is often these abandoned locations that can boast innovative cultural expression and a vibrant public sphere. Over the course of several years, the Urban Catalyst research team explored these temporary uses in European cities such as Amsterdam, Berlin, London and Rome.

Conversations with Architects
In the Age of Celebrity

Vladimir Belogolovsky
150 × 230 mm, 584 pages
180 images, softcover
ISBN 978-3-86922-299-8
€ 38.00

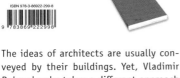

The ideas of architects are usually conveyed by their buildings. Yet, Vladimir Belogolovsky takes a different approach in his new work. The author gives a detailed picture of contemporary architects – through words. The publication presents interviews with thirty architects. The names of the interviewees read like a *Who-is-Who* of modern architecture. Their iconic work has attracted so much recent attention that it is often referred to as *Starchitecture*.

Tree Houses
Small Spaces in Nature

Andreas Wenning
225 × 280 mm, 304 pages
250 imageshardcover
ISBN 978-3-86922-410-7
€ 58.00 (third edition)

Treehouses offer a welcome release from everday routine by providing a sensual atmosphere close to nature. At the same time, the bold or idiosyncratic decor of a treehouse demonstrates the unique taste of its owner. The remote space amongst the trees represents a tranquil place for contemplation and rejuvenation. The third extended edition presents forty innovative examples of contemporary treehouses. With a review of the history and the cultural specificities of treehouses.

Africa Drawn
One Hundred Cities

Gary White / Marguerite Pienaar / Bouwer Serfontein
280 × 300 mm, 224 pages, 400 images
Hardcover, ISBN 978-3-86922-423-7
€ 48.00

Africa – a continent of small villages in the jungle and savannah? Certainly not. The urbanisation of the continent is advancing rapidly, while African cities are among the fastest growing in the world. *Africa Drawn* presents 100 of the most connected and important cities of the continent.

A visual feast of 300 images and masterfully drawn plans illustrates contemporary and historical place-making actions in Africa. The result is an artistic and visually fascinating documentation of African urban space and a convincing analysis of its structure and morphology.

26

ISBN 978-3-86922-456-5

384 pp.
1,370 imgs.
€ 78

**Competition Panels
and Diagrams**
Hossbach/Lehmhaus/
Eichelmann

ISBN 978-3-86922-217-2

416 pp.
500 imgs.
€ 78

Museum Buildings
Hans Wolfgang Hoffmann
Christian Schittich

ISBN 978-3-86922-415-2

320 pp.
570 imgs.
€ 88

Stadium Buildings
Martin Wimmer

ISBN 978-3-86922-427-5

416 pp.
700 imgs.
€ 78

Prefabricated Housing
Philipp Meuser
Spring 2017

ISBN 978-3-86922-515-9

240 pp.
300 imgs.
€ 38

**Container and
Modular Buildings**
Cornelia Dörries /
Sarah Zahradnik

ISBN 978-3-86922-414-5

Construction and
Design Manual
Drawing for Architects

240 pp.
350 imgs.
€ 68

Drawing for Architects
Natascha Meuser

ISBN 978-3-86922-535-7

Construction and
Design Manual
Drawing for Landscape Architects

Second edition

360 pp.
1,200 imgs.
€ 68

Drawing for Landscape Architects
Sabrina Wilk

ISBN 978-3-86922-417-6

Construction and
Design Manual
Architectural Diagrams 1

384 pp.
600 imgs.
€ 78

Architectural Diagrams 1
Miyoung Pyo

ISBN 978-3-86922-331-5

Construction and
Design Manual
Hotel Buildings

328 pp.
260 imgs.
€ 98

Hotel Buildings
Manfred Ronstedt /
Tobias Frey

ISBN 978-3-86922-237-0

Construction and
Design Manual
Offices

304 pp.
350 imgs.
€ 78

Offices
Ansgar Oswald

ISBN 978-3-86922-184-7

Construction and
Design Manual
Exhibition Halls

304 pp.
400 imgs.
€ 78

Exhibition Halls
Clemens F. Kusch

ISBN 978-3-86922-218-9

Construction and
Design Manual
Mobile Architecture

available again

844 pp.
700 imgs.
€ 78

Mobile Architecture
Kim Seonwook /
Pyo Miyoung

ISBN 978-3-86922-030-7

Townhouses Berlin

368 pp.
300 imgs.
€ 48

Townhouses Berlin
Hans Stimmann

ISBN 978-3-86922-038-3

Construction and
Design Manual
School Buildings

392 pp.
700 imgs.
€ 88

School Buildings
Natascha Meuser

5

ISBN 978-3-86922-170-0

Construction and
Design Manual
Accessible Architecture

304 pp.
300 imgs.
€ 78

Accessible Architecture
Philipp Meuser

ISBN 978-3-86922-177-9

Construction and
Design Manual
Medical Facilities and Health Care

304 pp.
500 imgs.
€ 78

Medical Facilities and Health Care
Philipp Meuser

ISBN 978-3-938666-54-8

Construction and
Design Manual
Medical Practices

available again

424 pp.
400 imgs.
€ 68

Medical Practices
Philipp Meuser

ISBN 978-3-86922-108-3

Construction and
Design Manual
Wayfinding and Signage

304 pp.
350 imgs.
€ 78

Wayfinding and Signage
Meuser/Pogade

ISBN 978-3-86922-194-6

Construction and
Design Manual
Architectural Photography

288 pp.
200 imgs.
€ 68

Architectural Photography
Axel Hausberg /
Anton Simons

ISBN 978-3-86922-109-0

Construction and
Design Manual
Architectural Renderings

464 pp.
350 imgs.
€ 48

Architectural Renderings
Fabio Schillaci

Architecture

ISBN 978-3-86922-358-2

198 pp.
190 imgs.
€ 28
en

Bangkok
Pattaranan Takkanon

ISBN 978-3-86922-547-0

192 pp.
400 imgs.
€ 18
en

Berlin
Dominik Schendel

ISBN 978-3-86922-394-0

418 pp.
700 imgs.
€ 38
en

Chile
Véronique Hours/
Fabien Mauduit

ISBN 978-3-86922-371-1

240 pp.
300 imgs.
€ 28
en

Dessau/Wörlitz
Bauhaus Dessau
Foundation/
Dessau-Wörlitz
Cultural Foundation

ISBN 978-3-86922-508-1

540 pp.
1,090 imgs.
€ 48
en

**United Arab
Emirates**
Bohle/Dimog

ISBN 978-3-86922-426-8

240 pp.
250 imgs.
€ 28
en

Wrocław
Marcin Szczelina

Sample pages

Wrocław

Chile

Berlin

Bangkok

224 pp.
400 imgs.
€ 38
en

Astana
Philipp Meuser

336 pp.
750 imgs.
€ 28
en

Brazil
Kimmel/
Tiggemann/
Santa Cecilia

400 pp.
700 imgs.
€ 48
en

China
Chakroff/Godel/
Gargus

400 pp.
450 imgs.
€ 38
en

Delhi
Anupam Bansal/
Malini Kochupillai

192 pp.
330 imgs.
€ 28
en

Hong Kong
Ulf Meyer

400 pp.
350 imgs.
€ 38
en

Indonesia
Imelda Akmal

552 pp.
750 imgs.
€ 38
en

Japan
Botond Bognar

300 pp.
350 imgs.
€ 38
en

Milan
Carlo Berizzi

300 pp.
350 imgs.
€ 38
it

Milano
Carlo Berizzi

368 pp.
350 imgs.
2 volumes
€ 38
en

Pyongyang
Philipp Meuser

400 pp.
800 imgs.
€ 48
en

Riga
Jānis Krastiņš

200 pp.
290 imgs.
€ 28
en/ru/ua

Slavutych
Ievgeniia Gubkina

176 pp.
700 imgs.
€ 28
en

South Africa
Nicholas Clarke/
Roger Fisher

268 pp.
350 imgs.
€ 28
en

Taiwan
Ulf Meyer

272 pp.
400 imgs.
€ 28
en

Tokyo
Ulf Meyer

232 pp.
420 imgs.
€ 38
en

Turin
Chiorino / Fassino /
Milan

NEW

232 pp.
420 imgs.
€ 38
it

Torino
Chiorino / Fassino /
Milan

280 pp.
400 imgs.
€ 38
en

Venice
Clemens F. Kusch/
Anabel Gelhaar

280 pp.
400 imgs.
€ 38
fr

Venise
Clemens F. Kusch/
Anabel Gelhaar

400 pp.
500 imgs.
€ 38
en

Yangon
Bansal/Fox/
Oka

ISBN 978-3-86922-406-0
ISBN 978-3-86922-220-2
ISBN 978-3-86922-348-3
ISBN 978-3-86922-167-0
ISBN 978-3-86922-201-1
ISBN 978-3-86922-425-1
ISBN 978-3-86922-193-9
ISBN 978-3-86922-396-4
ISBN 978-3-86922-397-1
ISBN 978-3-86922-187-8
ISBN 978-3-86922-286-8
ISBN 978-3-86922-424-4
ISBN 978-3-86922-262-2
ISBN 978-3-86922-145-8
ISBN 978-3-86922-173-1
ISBN 978-3-86922-411-4
ISBN 978-3-86922-553-1
ISBN 978-3-86922-362-9
ISBN 978-3-86922-377-3
ISBN 978-3-86922-375-9

Behind the Iron Curtain
Confession of a
Soviet Architect
Felix Novikov
252 pp.
360 imgs.
€ 28
ISBN 978-3-86922-359-9

**Conversations with
Peter Eisenman**
The Evolution of
Architectural Style
Vladimir Belogolovsky
152 pp.
130 imgs.
€ 28
ISBN 978-3-86922-531-9

Space Race Archaeologies
Photographs, Biographies,
and Design
Pedro Ignacio Alonso
128 pp.
130 imgs.
€ 28
ISBN 978-3-86922-537-1

Seismic Modernism
Architecture and Housing
in Soviet Tashkent
Philipp Meuser
256 pp.
300 imgs.
€ 28
ISBN 978-3-86922-493-0

Design for Space
Soviet and Russian
Mission Patches
Alexander Glushko
244 pp.
600 imgs.
€ 28
ISBN 978-3-86922-328-5

Belyayevo Forever
A Soviet Microrayon on its
Way to the UNESCO List
Kuba Snopek
192 pp.
130 imgs.
€ 28
ISBN 978-3-86922-438-1

**The Morphology
of the Times**
European Cities and
their Historical Growth
Ton Hinse
304 pp.
400 imgs.
€ 28
ISBN 978-3-86922-309-4

Berlin Urban Design
A Brief History of a
European City
Harald Bodenschatz
182 pp.
160 imgs.
€ 28
ISBN 978-3-86922-105-2

City and Wind
Climate as an
Architectural Instrument
Krautheim/Pasel/Pfeiffer/
Schultz-Granberg
208 pp.
274 imgs.
€ 28
ISBN 978-3-86922-310-0

Sergey Chernyshev
Architect of
The New Moscow
Ivan Lykoshin/
Irina Cheredina
264 pp.
290 imgs.
€ 28
ISBN 978-3-86922-314-8

Galina Balashova
Architect of the Soviet
Space Programme
Phiipp Meuser
160 pp.
189 imgs.
€ 28
ISBN 978-3-86922-355-1

Moshe Zarhy
Health Facilities in Israel
Peter R. Pawlik
380 pp.
300 imgs.
€ 28
ISBN 978-3-86922-340-7

Felix Novikov
Architect of the
Soviet Modernism
Vladimir Belogolovsky
176 pp.
250 imgs.
€ 28
ISBN 978-3-86922-289-9

Yakov Chernikhov
Architectural
Fantasies in Russian
Constructivism
Dmitry Khmelnitsky
144 pp.
193 imgs.
€ 28
ISBN 978-3-86922-281-3

Sergey Chernyshev
Architect of
The New Moscow
Ivan Lykoshin/
Irina Cheredina
264 pp.
290 imgs.
€ 28
ISBN 978-3-86922-314-8

DOM publishers' editorial team in Dessau in July 2016.

Enriching Books and Buildings

Our publishing programme combines both of our passions, namely architecture and designing high-quality books. Since 2005, we have been publishing premium books on architecture and design, as well as architectural journals. Experienced editors, graphic designers and architects all work together at the interface of theory and practice. We hope that you will take the time to browse our extensive programme and would be pleased to hear any suggestions or critical comments you may have. Similarly, if you have an idea for a book simply get in touch.

DOM publishers
Caroline-von-Humboldt-Weg 20
10117 Berlin, Germany
T +49. 30. 20 69 69 30
F +49. 30. 20 69 69 32
info@dom-publishers.com

Orders in the Webshop

You can place orders for books and card games in our Webshop. Deliveries take place within three to four days (Europe) and five to fifteen days (overseas).

www.dom-publishers.com

Our General Terms and Conditions of Business are published on the Internet on *www.dom-publishers.com*
The publisher reserves the right to change the layout and content of the titles before they appear.

Printed in September 2016
Publisher: Dr.-Ing. Philipp Meuser
© DOM publishers 2016

STOP IT! THERE'S NOTHING FUNNY ABOUT ARCHITECTURE!

DOM publishers
on Facebook

Books made by Architects
www.dom-publishers.com

Distribution

Germany/Austria
DOM publishers
Contact: Sabine Hofmann
Roethenweg 15
96152 Burghaslach, Germany
T +49. 9552. 93 10 12
F +49. 9552. 93 10 11
sabine.hofmann@dom-publishers.com

USA and Canada
Ingram Publisher Services (IPS)
1210 Ingram Drive
Chambersburg, PA 17202, USA
T +1. 855. 867-1918
F +1. 800. 838-1149

Sales

**Benelux Union, France, Greece,
Italy, Portugal, Spain**
Flavio Marcello
Via Belzoni 12
35121 Padova, Italy
T +39. 049. 836 06 71
F +39. 049. 878 67 59
marcello@marcellosas.it

UK and Northern Ireland
RIBA Bookshops and Distribution
15 Bonhill Street
London EC2P 2EA
T +44. 20. 72 56 72 22
F +44. 20. 73 74 85 00
orders@ribabooks.com

Scandinavia and Finland
Elisabeth Harder-Kreimann
Joachim-Mähl-Straße 28
22459 Hamburg, Germany
T +49. 40. 5554 04 46
F +49. 40. 5554 04 44
elisabeth@harder-kreimann.de

Estonia, Latvia, Lithuania
David Towle International
PO Box 3300
13603 Stockholm, Sweden
T +46. 8. 777 3962
david@dti.a.se

India
Mehul Book Sales/Ketan Khandor
Kitab Mahal, 192 - Dr. D. N. Road
Fort, Mumbai 400001
T +91. 22. 22 05 40 44
F + 91. 22. 22 06 06 94
info@mehulbooksales.com

China
Benjamin Pan
Ro. 2804, Building #1, No. 77, Lane 569
Xinhua Road, Changning District
Shanghai 200052
T +86. 21. 54259557
benjamin.pan@cpmarketing.com.cn

USA and Canada
Actar D, Inc./Brian Brash
151 Grand St, 5th FL
New York, NY 10013
T +1. 212. 966-2207
F +1. 212. 966-2214
brian.brash@actar-d.com

Latin America
Nicolas Friedmann
Representaciones Editoriales
Rbla. Badal 64, Ent. 1
08014 Barcelona, Spain
T +34. 637. 455006
F +34. 93. 4217310
nicolasfriedmann@gmail.com

DOM
publishers